Susan Burt
Pattley Bridge
Aug. 2003.

THE ILLUSTRATED
GERTRUDE JEKYLL

COLOUR SCHEMES FOR THE FLOWER GARDEN

Gertrude Jekyll

Illustrations by Charlotte Wess

WINDWARD · FRANCES LINCOLN

Frances Lincoln Limited
4 Torriano Mews, Torriano Avenue
London NW5 2RZ

British Library Cataloguing-in-Publication Data
A catalogue record for this book is available from the British Library

ISBN 0 7112 1792 0

Printed in Hong Kong by
Kwong Fat Offset Printing Co. Ltd

First Frances Lincoln edition 1988
First paperback edition 2001

3 5 7 9 8 6 4 2

CONTENTS

PREFACE

Colour Schemes for the Flower Garden, first published in 1914, was the twelfth of fifteen books written by Gertrude Jekyll, but it had a long pedigree. In 1882 Miss Jekyll wrote an article on 'Colour in the Flower Garden' for William Robinson's magazine *The Garden*. A longer essay of the same title appeared as a chapter in Robinson's momentous *English Flower Garden* in 1883. Miss Jekyll's own books, beginning with *Wood and Garden* in 1899, made constant reference to colour and colour planning, and in 1908 *Colour in the Flower Garden* was published, her ninth book in as many years. In 1914 a new edition was published as *Colour Schemes for the Flower Garden*, under which title it ran through six editions before Miss Jekyll's death in 1932.

Colour Schemes is probably her best-known book and is undoubtedly one of the most influential gardening books of the twentieth century. Sadly, its very success has often damaged rather than enhanced Miss Jekyll's reputation: her writing flows with such deceptive ease that readers have too often drifted along with the prose, unwittingly absorbing and perpetuating a series of half-truths. The life-long experience compressed into *Colour Schemes* is glibly and quite inaccurately represented as a policy of dividing up the garden into a string of compartments, each containing pastel-coloured herbaceous borders offering only a brief season of interest.

Miss Jekyll's own philosophy, constantly reiterated, was that 'if something is worth doing, it is worth doing well'. Her books were written with painstaking care and, although they do make easy bedtime reading, there is much more pleasure and profit to be derived from reading them with equal care.

Her greatest contribution to English culture was to reassert the position of gardening as a fine art. In the eighteenth century, painting, poetry and gardening had been personified as the three most important Muses, with gardening widely accepted as the greatest art and a constant source of inspiration for the other two. Miss Jekyll saw as a painter, she wrote as a poet and she sought, through her writing, to re-establish for gardening the position from which it had fallen

9

during the horticultural turmoil of the nineteenth century.

Gertrude Jekyll was born in 1843 in London but spent most of her life in Surrey – at Bramley, where she spent her childhood, and at Munstead, where she lived first with her mother in Munstead House and then, for the last thirty-five years of her life, in her own house at Munstead Wood. In 1861, at the age of seventeen, she returned to London to study art and design in the School of Art in South Kensington. With customary zeal she immersed herself in the study of botany and ornamentation, colour theory and art history. Chevreul's *The Law of Simultaneous Contrast of Colours* and Ruskin's *Modern Painters* were constant companions and Miss Jekyll spent many hours in the National Gallery copying the works of Turner catalogued by Ruskin. This early training endowed her with a profound understanding of colour and its effects. Certainly Turner's use of colour had a lasting and wide-ranging effect on Miss Jekyll's gardening and nowhere is this more obvious than in her preference for planting in broad harmonious gradations of colour. Her greatest ability as an artist-gardener was in her recognition of the value of harmony – and the importance of the contrast without which harmony degenerates into monotony. It has been suggested that the colour scheme of her main flower border at Munstead Wood was inspired by Turner's painting *The Fighting Téméraire*, although its colour sequence from glowing sunset through the inky purples of the dark water to golden reflection is reversed in the flower border.

The main border began and ended with cool blue and purple flowers set in a haze of grey foliage, and the grey-leaved rue had a special place in such groups: the appearance of its sharp yellow flowers gave added clarity to the blue of delphiniums and the purple-blue of campanulas. In the middle of the border 'the colour is strong and gorgeous': strong yellows, scarlets and crimsons built in a crescendo with dark-leaved cannas, dahlias and antirrhinums at the fiery core, but here and there a cloud of gypsophila simultaneously lightened and brightened the effect. Those clouds of gypsophila settled down on the border had a wonderful softness, but the softness was accentuated by the gladiolus shooting up spires of red flowers nearby. In other strong-coloured groupings a thin drift of white lilies shone forth to prevent the richness from becoming heavy and dull.

While in London Miss Jekyll also met William Morris, the leading figure in the Arts and Crafts Movement, and she found in Morris' teaching and practice a mirror of her own attitude to life. For Miss Jekyll art, craft and life were part of an inseparable whole; tradition was a stimulus to creativity and creativity must be cherished as the gift of a beneficent creator. 'Sense of beauty is the gift of God, for which those who have received it in good measure can never be thankful enough.'

Gertrude Jekyll's talents were many. Painting was her main love, but she enjoyed wood-carving, silverwork, tapestry, embroidery and, later, the photography with which she illustrated her books. Her other enduring interest was, of course, her garden – a work of art, a scene of cultivation and the setting for a comfortable but simple existence. She rarely spoke of 'garden design', but rather of gardening: it was through a knowledge of plants and their requirements, the craft of cultivation, and the art of composing them purposefully that the garden evolved, not through some brief skirmish at the drawing-board.

In *Colour Schemes* art and craft are inextricably combined. In one part of the garden the catmint which provided the only flower among grey patches of stachys and lavender was carefully dead-headed as soon as it began to fade, encouraging a second flush of flower for the border's main season in August. In another part that same welcome flower was cut back later so that its second flowering coincided with the Michaelmas daisies in September. The staking up, tying down and dropping in of plants necessary to maintain the scheme of the main border in late summer required – and received – as much dexterity with the secateur and spade as Miss Jekyll displayed with her scissors and needles in tapestry, patchwork or embroidery, or her chisels in the carving of vine-leaves for her wine-cellar door.

In the realm of gardening Miss Jekyll has made three major contributions. First and foremost, she was an artist-gardener of prodigious ability, observing plants in their finest details and composing them into beautiful pictures. Secondly, by her influence on Edwin Lutyens (who designed her house at Munstead Wood) and her informal partnership with him, she resolved the bitter dispute between architects and gardeners as to who should design gardens. It was not a matter for architects *or* gardeners but for architects *and* gardeners: the firm composition of Lutyens' stonework with the luxuriant but disciplined sympathetic planting by Miss Jekyll provided the inspiration for a new wave of English gardens at Hidcote, Tintinhull, Sissinghurst and elsewhere. Thirdly, Miss Jekyll recorded her ideas and her experience in a series of books in which prose merges imperceptibly into poetry. These remain, long after the garden at Munstead Wood has disappeared, to inspire successive generations of gardeners.

Interestingly the first page of her first book, *Wood and Garden*, declares 'I lay no claim either to literary ability or to botanical knowledge'. This was not false modesty but a genuine recognition of the hard work required to achieve success in any endeavour. At first glance her writing may seem over-stuffed with words, as deceptively casual as her abundant flower borders. In reality each word, like each plant, was chosen to convey exactly the right effect: the book, the chapter, the phrase are each carefully composed.

The atmospheric opening phrases of *Colour Schemes* describing the woodland in March leads into the first colour grouping: a 'straggling group' of *Daphne mezereum*, some 'clumps' of red Lent hellebores and some 'half-connected patches' of the common dog-tooth violet, simple but evocative wording. Elsewhere Miss Jekyll speaks of 'thin streams' of white tulips, of 'pink clouds' of London pride with the white stars of St Bruno's lily 'shooting up' among it. White foxgloves 'spire up' among the birches, while for her border planting she described the practical and artistic reasons for her planting methods by adapting another word: 'Many years ago I came to the conclusion that in all flower borders it is better to plant in long rather than block-shaped patches. It not only has a more pictorial effect, but a long thin planting does not leave an unsightly empty space when the flowers are done and the leaves have perhaps died down. The word "drift" conveniently describes the shape I have in mind, and I commonly use it in speaking of these long-shaped plantings.'

Colour Schemes for the Flower Garden is not all about colour. Indeed, it is worth remembering that the original was illustrated by over 100 photographs in black and white. Rather it is about the role of colour, in relation to other attributes of plants, in the making of gardens. It begins with the subtle beauty of late-winter woodland and the effect of wind and sun on the picture. It continues with descriptions of scattered patches of colour from sad hellebores to brilliant forsythia against a blue sky. Spring flowers are gradually orchestrated into the brilliant sparkle of early bulbs, followed by the increasing riches of the

June garden and the splendid climax of the main flower border in high summer. The splendour then fades to the subtle colouring of fruits and the soft, misty colours of the winter landscape. Relieving the grand scheme of the main text are incidental – but important – chapters on bedding plants, on wood and shrubbery edges, on plants in pots and on walls. The book is as carefully planned as the main border itself, beginning with soft colours, building to a gorgeous climax and fading again to a misty close, with occasional glimpses into other parts of the garden, related but different.

Careful reading of *Colour Schemes* should dispel the two most common misunderstandings about Gertrude Jekyll's gardening.

The first is that she turned to gardening because her worsening eyesight prevented her painting and that she therefore saw the garden only as a vague blur of colours. Although her eyesight was both poor and painful, she observed in minute detail and with great accuracy. Her description of the great Scots pine trunk in the woodland (pages 36–38) is typical of such observations. The main flower border at Munstead Wood was, of course, designed to be seen as a grand composition: 'Looked at from a little way forward, for a wide space of grass allows this point of view, the whole border can be seen as one picture, the cool colouring at the ends enhancing the brilliant warmth of the middle.' But it also invited closer inspection to reveal a series of picturesque incidents, each one 'of such a colouring that it prepares the eye, in accordance with natural law, for what is to follow.' For visitors with sharper sensitivity there was delight in still finer details – the velvety texture of crimson antirrhinums, the sooty eye of the delphinium flowers, the dark stems of *Aster divaricatus* or the recurving tips of the striped *Miscanthus*.

The second misunderstanding overemphasizes the importance of the hardy flower border in Miss Jekyll's gardening: the stereotyped view of her gardens as comprising separate compartments of colour-planned flower borders, each interesting for a brief period of the year and dull thereafter. There were colour borders at Munstead Wood, especially the main border, and they were designed *primarily* to be of interest over one to three months, but Miss Jekyll's philosophy was that nothing should be ugly and that no idea should be pursued beyond the bounds of common sense. 'It is a curious thing that people will sometimes spoil some garden project for the sake of a word. . . . Surely

13

the business of the blue garden is to be beautiful as well as to be blue. My own idea is that it should be beautiful first, and then just as blue as may be consistent with its best possible beauty.'

At Munstead Wood the staking was invisible, an iron-roofed toolshed was covered with sedums, and borders were planned to be attractive, even if not colourful, over the longest possible period.

The main border had a backdrop of evergreens with wintersweet, laurustinus and magnolia flowers in winter and early spring. There were also generous clumps of grey foliage and soft lavender flowers long before the main season, with orange poppies as a focal point. The border of early bulbs had a backbone of evergreen ferns and an edging of mossy saxifrage for the winter. Hellebores and bergenias provided muted flower colour before the brilliant sequence of bulbs began. At its peak the vivid yellow leaves of valerian were used as a stunning contrast to blue hyacinths and scillas, while harmonizing with the sharp yellow daffodils. Miss Jekyll also mentions a clump of day-lily, valuable for its early pale green sword-like foliage − but that same clump was on the centreline of the path into the June garden. Its orange flowers formed a striking point of colour seen from the window of the Hut and a warm echo of the poppies and lilies of the June Garden border. The Spring Garden captured all the grace and delicacy of spring flowers but was backed by a large group of yucca, *Euphorbia wulfenii*, acanthus and kniphofia − a durable tapestry of leaf forms, and a striking composition of white, deep purple and flaming orange spires seen in late summer across a sea of green from the much-frequented west entrance to the garden. These important points of interest tied the whole garden together.

Recurrent groups and drifts of good foliage plants reinforced the sense of unity between garden compartments. Yuccas, euphorbias, veratrum, myrrhis, bergenia, hellebore and hosta were used throughout the garden, but not indiscriminately, to create the balance between harmony and variety central to Miss Jekyll's design.

The compartments at Munstead Wood were not isolated entities, then, but part of a greater whole, bound together in subtle but deliberate ways. The main border could be seen as a whole, as a series of parts or as a myriad of details. Equally it formed part of a larger composition. It was an integral part of the cluster of flower borders. The cluster merged into its woodland setting and views extended from the woodland to the surrounding hills. 'The lovely colour of the distant winter landscape' and the storms watched from the Thunder House in a corner of the kitchen garden were essential parts of the garden's plan.

One effect of these twin misunderstandings is to create a third. There is a widespread belief that what Miss Jekyll wrote is only relevant to the large garden maintained by a large team of gardeners. Nothing could be further from the truth. She stressed repeatedly that the size of a garden has very little to do with its merit. 'It is the size of the owner's heart and brain and goodwill that will make his garden either delightful or dull.' Her own 15-acre garden was not big enough for her. She desired a long, rocky hillside to plant with broad masses of phlomis, lavender, rosemary, cistus and *Othonnopsis*. She longed for the space and resources to create a blue garden and a green garden, but she was not dismayed by limitations of space and time. She composed, on a smaller scale, the dry wall of grey-leaved plants near the Hut and the blue groups in her main flower border.

The artistry and painstaking craftsmanship evident in her work-shop, the studio, the garden and her books were all humble responses to the Grand Design, works of praise from a gardener who would have liked much more but was serenely satisfied and thankful for what she had. The main flower border at Munstead Wood was 200 feet long and 14 feet deep, but Miss Jekyll took great care, too, with the planning of a group of pots in the north courtyard of the house or the draping of a clematis swag. She derived delight from the miniscule composition of a strand of wild clematis, a wayward tuft of campanula and an edging of thyme creeping out of the lawn to decorate the garden step. Her writing is an inspiration for people with gardens on any scale from stately home to window box.

This new edition of *Colour Schemes* not only preserves the quality of Gertrude Jekyll's writing, but also enhances it, with illustrations in colour of many of the plants and plant associations she used and photographs of gardens that successfully reinterpret her ideas. Again it is important to reiterate that there is more to be gained than mere recipes for colour grouping. One of the most poetic moments in the book occurs in describing, not the gorgeousness of the main border, but the woodland in spring: 'Growing close to the ground in a tuft of dark-green moss, is an interesting plant – *Goodyera repens*, a terrestrial

15

orchid. One might easily pass it by, for its curiously white-veined leaves are half hidden in the moss, and its spike of pale greenish-white flower is not conspicuous; but knowing it is there, I never pass without kneeling down, both to admire its beauty and also to ensure its well-being by a careful removal of a little of the deep moss here and there where it threatens too close an invasion.' This unaffected blend of observation, contemplation and cultivation, an English equivalent of the oriental influence which later had a radical influence on the design of modern gardens, offers a lesson to us all of the joy to be derived from the pursuit of gardening as a fine art and from the careful reading of this, Gertrude Jekyll's most important book.

Richard Bisgrove
University of Reading
October 1987

INTRODUCTION

To plant and maintain a flower border, *with a good scheme for colour*, is by no means the easy thing that is commonly supposed.

I believe that the only way in which it can be made successful is to devote certain borders to certain times of year; each border or garden region to be bright for from one to three months.

Nothing seems to me more unsatisfactory than the border that in spring shows a few patches of flowering bulbs in ground otherwise looking empty, or with tufts of herbaceous plants just coming through. Then the bulbs die down, and their place is wanted for something that comes later. Either the ground will then show bare patches, or the place of the bulbs will be forgotten and they will be cruelly stabbed by fork or trowel when it is wished to put something in the apparently empty space.

For many years I have been working at these problems in my own garden, and, having come to certain conclusions, can venture to put them forth with some confidence. I may mention that from the nature of the ground, in its original state partly wooded and partly bare field, and from its having been brought into cultivation and some sort of shape before it was known where the house now upon it would exactly stand, the garden has less general unity of design than I should have wished. The position and general form of its various portions were accepted mainly according to their natural conditions, so that the garden ground, though but of small extent, falls into different regions, with a general, but not altogether definite, cohesion.

I am strongly of opinion that the possession of a quantity of plants, however good the plants may be themselves and however ample their number, does not make a garden; it only makes a *collection*. Having got the plants, the great thing is to use them with careful selection and definite intention. Merely having them, or having them planted unassorted in garden spaces, is only like having a box of paints from the best colourman, or, to go one step further, it is like having portions of these paints set out upon a palette. This does not constitute a picture; and it seems to me that the duty we owe to our gardens and to our own bettering in our gardens is so to use the plants that they shall form beautiful pictures; and that, while delighting our eyes they should be always training those eyes to a more exalted criticism; to a state of mind and artistic conscience that will not tolerate bad or careless combination or any sort of misuse of plants, but in which it becomes a point of honour to be always striving for the best.

It is just in the way it is done that lies the whole difference between commonplace gardening and gardening that may rightly claim to rank as a fine art. Given the same space of ground and the same material, they may either be fashioned into a dream of beauty, a place of perfect rest and refreshment of mind and body – a series of soul-satisfying pictures – a treasure of well-set jewels; or they may be so misused that everything is jarring and displeasing. To learn how to perceive the difference and how to do right is to apprehend gardening as a fine art. In practice it is to place every plant or group of plants with such thoughtful care and definite intention that they shall form a part of a harmonious whole, and that successive portions, or in some cases even single details, shall show a series of pictures. It is so to regulate the trees and undergrowth of the wood that their lines and masses come into beautiful form and harmonious proportion; it is to be always watching, noting and doing, and putting oneself meanwhile into closest acquaintance and sympathy with the growing things.

In this spirit, the garden and woodland, such as they are, have been formed. There have been many failures, but, every now and then, I am encouraged and rewarded by a certain measure of success. Yet, as the critical faculty becomes keener, so does the standard of aim rise higher; and, year by year, the desired point seems always to elude attainment.

But, as I may perhaps have taken more trouble in working out certain problems, and given more thought to methods of arranging growing flowers, especially in ways of colour-combination, than amateurs in general, I have thought that it may be helpful to some of them to describe as well as I can by word, and to show by plan and picture, what I have tried to do, and to point out where I have succeeded and where I have failed.

I must ask my kind readers not to take it amiss if I mention here that I cannot undertake to show it them on the spot. I am a solitary worker; I am growing old and tired, and suffer from very bad and painful sight. My garden is my workshop, my private study and place of rest. For the sake of health and reasonable enjoyment of life it is necessary to keep it quite private, and to refuse the many applications of those who offer it visits. My oldest friends can now only be admitted. So I ask my readers to spare me the painful task of writing long letters of excuse and explanation; a task that has come upon me almost daily of late years in the summer months, that has sorely tried my weak and painful eyes, and has added much to the difficulty of getting through an already over-large correspondence.

Chapter I

A MARCH STUDY

THERE comes a day towards the end of March when there is but little wind, and that is from the west or even south-west. The sun has gained much power, so that it is pleasant to sit out in the garden, or, better still, in some sunny nook of sheltered woodland. There is such a place among silver-trunked birches, with here and there the splendid richness of masses of dark holly. The rest of the background above eye-level is of the warm bud-colour of the summer-leafing trees, and, below, the fading rust of the now nearly flattened fronds of last year's bracken, and the still paler drifts of leaves from neighbouring oaks and chestnuts. The sunlight strikes brightly on the silver stems of the birches, and casts their shadows clear-cut across the grassy woodland ride. The grass is barely green as yet, but has the faint winter green of herbage not yet grown and still powdered with the short remnants of the fine-leaved, last-year-mown heath grasses. Brown leaves still hang on young beech and oak. The trunks of the Spanish chestnuts are elephant-grey, a notable contrast to the sudden, vivid shafts of the birches. Some groups of the pale early Pyrenean daffodil gleam level on the ground a little way forward.

It is the year's first complete picture of flower-effect in the woodland landscape. The place is not very far from the house, within the nearest hundred yards of the copse, where flowers seem to be more in place than further away. Looking to the left, the long ridge and south slope of the house-roof is seen through the leafless trees, though the main wall-block is hidden by the sheltering hollies and junipers.

Coming down towards the garden by another broad grassy way, that goes westward through the chestnuts and then turns towards the down-hill north, there comes yet another deviation through rhododendrons and birches to the main lawn. But before the last turn there is a pleasant mass of colour showing in the wood-edge on the dead-leaf carpet. It is a straggling group of *Daphne mezereum*, with some clumps of red Lent hellebores, and, to the front, some half-connected patches

'A flower picture of warm white and finest yellow': a combination of *Magnolia stellata*, 'whose milk-white flowers may be counted by the thousand' and the fresh, gold-rimmed foliage of *Euonymus fortunei* 'Silver Queen' epitomizes the beauty of spring. The white narcissus 'Tresamble' and yellow erythroniums extend the scheme to the woodland floor.

21

Left to right: Red lent hellebore, *Daphne mezereum*, dog-tooth violet.

of the common dog-tooth violet. The nearly related combination of colour is a delight to the trained colour-eye. There is nothing brilliant; it is all restrained – refined; in harmony with the veiled light that reaches the flowers through the great clumps of hollies and tall half-overhead chestnuts and neighbouring beech. The colours are all a little 'sad', as the old writers so aptly say of the flower-tints of secondary strength. But it is a perfect picture. One comes to it again and again as one does to any picture that is good to live with.

To devise these living pictures from simple well-known flowers seems to me the best thing to do in gardening. Whether it is the putting together of two or three kinds of plants, or even of one kind only in some happy setting, or whether it is the ordering of a much larger number of plants, as in a flower-border of middle and late summer, the intention is always the same. Whether the arrangement is simple and modest, whether it is bold and gorgeous, whether it is obvious or whether it is subtle, the aim is always to use the plants to the best of one's means and intelligence so as to form pictures of living beauty.

It is a thing that I see so rarely attempted, and that seems to me so important, that the wish to suggest it to others, and to give an idea of examples that I have worked out, in however modest a way, is the purpose of this book.

These early examples within the days of March are of special interest because as yet flowers are but few ; the mind is less distracted by much variety than later in the year, and is more readily concentrated on the few things that may be done and observed ; so that the necessary restriction is a good preparation, by easy steps, for the wider field of observation that is presented later.

Now we pass on through the dark masses of rhododendron and the birches that shoot up among them. How the silver stems, blotched and banded with varied browns and greys so deep in tone that they show like a luminous black, tell among the glossy rhododendron green ; and how strangely different is the way of growth of the two kinds of tree ; the tall white trunks spearing up through the dense, dark, leathery leaf-masses of solid, roundish outline, with their delicate network of reddish branch and spray gently swaying far overhead !

Now we come to the lawn, which slopes a little downward to the north. On the right it has a low retaining-wall, whose top line is level ; it bears up a border and pathway next the house's western face. The border and wall are all of a piece, for it is a dry wall partly planted with the same shrubby and half-shrubby things that are in the earth above. They have been comforting to look at all the winter ; a pleasant grey coating of *Phlomis*, lavender, rosemary, *Cistus*, and *Santolina* ; and at the end and angle where the wall is highest, a mass of *Chaenomeles japonica,* planted both above and below, already showing its rose-red bloom. At one point at the foot of the wall is a strong tuft of *Iris unguicularis* whose first blooms appeared in November. This capital plant flowers bravely all through the winter in any intervals of open weather. It likes a sunny place against a wall in poor soil. If it is planted in better ground the leaves grow very tall and it gives but little bloom.

Now we pass among some shrub-clumps, and at the end come upon a cheering sight ; a tree of *Magnolia denudata* bearing hundreds of its great white cups of fragrant bloom. Just before reaching it, and taking part with it in the garden picture, are some tall bushes of *Forsythia suspensa*, tossing out many-feet-long branches loaded with their burden

23

of clear yellow flowers. They are ten to twelve feet high, and one looks up at much of the bloom clear-cut against the pure blue of the sky ; the upper part of the magnolia also shows against the sky. Here there is a third flower-picture ; this time of warm white and finest yellow on brilliant blue, and out in open sunlight. Among the forsythias is also a large bush of *Magnolia stellata*, whose milk-white flowers may be counted by the thousand. As the earlier *M. denudata* goes out of bloom it comes into full bearing, keeping pace with the forsythia, whose season runs on well into April.

It is always a little difficult to find suitable places for the early bulbs. Many of them can be enjoyed in rough and grassy places, but we also want to combine them into pretty living pictures in the garden proper.

Nothing seems to me more unsatisfactory than the usual way of having them scattered about in small patches in the edges of flower-borders, where they only show as little disconnected dabs of colour, and where they are necessarily in danger of disturbance and probable injury when their foliage has died down and their places are wanted for summer flowers.

It was a puzzle for many years to know how to treat these early bulbs, but at last a plan was devised that seems so satisfactory that I have no hesitation in advising it for general adoption.

On the further side of a path that bounds my June garden is a border about seventy feet long and ten feet wide. At every ten feet along the back is a larch post planted with a free-growing rose. These are not only to clothe their posts, but to grow into garlands swinging on slack chains from post to post. Beyond are bamboos, and then an old hedge-bank with Scots pines, oaks, thorns, &c. The border slopes upwards from the path, forming a bank of gentle ascent. It was first planted

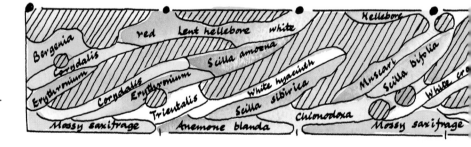

The bank of early bulbs. Groups of ferns shown by diagonal hatching

24

with hardy ferns in bold drifts ; male fern for the most part, because it is not only handsome but extremely persistent, the fronds remaining green into the winter. Between the drifts of ferns come the bulbs, with a general edging to the front of mossy saxifrage.

The colour scheme begins with the pink of *Bergenia ligulata*, and with the lower-toned pinks of *Corydalis solida* and the dog-tooth violets (*Erythronium*). At the back of these are Lent hellebores of dull red colouring, agreeing charmingly with the colour of the bulbs. A few white Lent hellebores are at the end ; they have turned to greenish white by the time the rather late *Scilla amoena* is in bloom. Then comes a brilliant patch of pure blue with white – *Scilla sibirica* and white hyacinths, followed by the also pure blues of *Scilla bifolia* and *Chionodoxa* and the later, more purple blue of grape hyacinth. A long drift of white crocus comes next, in beauty in the border's earliest days ; and later, the blue-white of *Puschkinia* ; then again pure blue and white of *Chionodoxa* and white hyacinth.

Now the colours change to white and yellow and golden foliage, with the bicolour trumpet daffodil *Narcissus* 'Princeps', and beyond it the stronger yellow of two other small early kinds – *N. nanus* and the charming little *N. minor*, quite distinct though so often confounded with *N. nanus* in gardens[1]. With these, and in other strips and patches towards the end of the border, are plantings of the golden valerian, so useful for its bright yellow foliage quite early in the year. The leaves of the orange day-lily are also of a pale yellowish-green colour when they first come up, and are used at the end of the border. These plants of golden and pale foliage are also placed in a further region beyond the plan, and show to great advantage as the eye enfilades the border and reaches the more distant places. Before the end of the bulb-border is reached there is once more a drift of harmonized faint pink colouring

Top right: *Scilla sibirica*; bottom left: *Chionodoxa luciliae*.

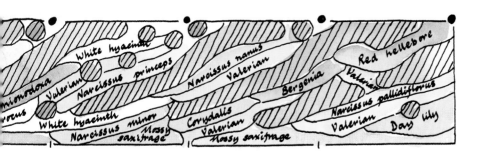

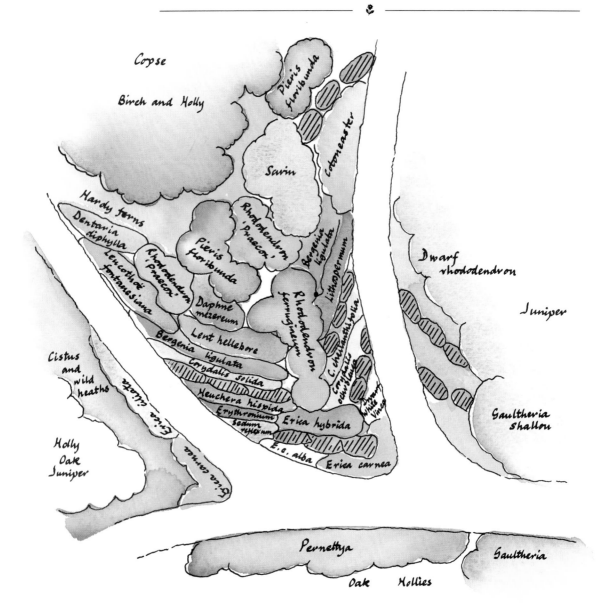

From lawn to copse

of bergenia and the little corydalis with the pale early Pyrenean daffodil, *Narcissus pallidiflorus*[2].

The bulb-flowers are not all in bloom exactly at the same time, but there is enough of the colour intended to give the right effect in each grouping. Standing at the end, just beyond the dog-tooth violets, the arrangement and progression of colour is pleasant and interesting, and in some portions vivid; the pure blues in the middle spaces being

26

much enhanced by the yellow flowers and golden foliage that follow.

A nearly similar arrangement of flowers for earliest spring has been made at a place where a path from the lawn branches into three grassy ways up into the copse. The planted promontory is a bank rising from the grass paths and is set with a few large stones. As it is backed by hollies and junipers, and then by the birches of the wood, it has a back planting of such shrubs as both accord in colour with the flowering plants and lead suitably to the further woodland. These are *Rhododendron* × *praecox* and *Pieris floribunda* – a wide-spreading savin is already behind them – while the front planting is stiffened by some of the early blooming heaths, *Erica herbacea* in one or two colourings and *E. hybrida*. There is also, though the bloom will not be till later, a kind of backbone of alpenrose (*Rhododendron ferrugineum*), which gives a certain aspect of strength and solidity.

Through April and May the leaves of the bulbs are growing tall, and their seed-pods are carefully removed to prevent exhaustion. By the end of May the ferns are throwing up their leafy crooks ; by June the feathery fronds are displayed in all their tender freshness ; they spread over the whole bank, and we forget that there are any bulbs between. By the time the June garden, whose western boundary it forms, has come into fullest bloom it has become a completely furnished bank of fern-beauty.

Chapter II

THE WOOD

TEN acres is but a small area for a bit of woodland, yet it can be made apparently much larger by well-considered treatment. As the years pass and different portions answer to careful guidance, I am myself surprised to see the number and wonderful variety of the pictures of sylvan beauty that it displays throughout the year. I did not specially aim at variety, but, guided by the natural conditions of each region, tried to think out how best they might be fostered and perhaps a little bettered.

The only way in which variety of aspect was deliberately chosen was in the way of thinning out the natural growths. It was a wood of seedling trees that had come up naturally after an old wood of Scots pine had been cut down, and it seemed well to clear away all but one, or in some cases two kinds of trees in the several regions. Even in this the intention was to secure simplicity rather than variety, so that in moving about the ground there should be one thing at a time to see and enjoy. It is just this quality of singleness or simplicity of aim that I find wanting in gardens in general, where one may see quantities of the best plants grandly grown and yet no garden pictures.

Of course one has to remember that there are many minds to which this need of an artist's treatment of garden and woodland does not appeal, just as there are some who do not care for music or for poetry, or who see no difference between the sculpture of the old Greeks and that of any modern artist who is not of the first rank, or to whom architectural refinement is as an unknown language. And in the case of the more superficial enjoyment of flowers one has sympathy too. For a love of flowers, of any kind, however shallow, is a sentiment that makes for human sympathy and kindness, and is in itself uplifting, as everything must be that is a source of reverence and admiration. Still, the object of this book is to draw attention, however slightly and imperfectly, to the better ways of gardening, and to bring to bear upon the subject some consideration of that combination of common sense with sincerity of purpose, sense of beauty, and artistic knowledge that can make plain ground and growing things into a year-long succession of living pictures.

Common sense I put first, because it restrains from any sort of folly or sham or affectation. Sense of beauty is the gift of God, for which those who have received it in good measure can never be thankful enough. The nurturing of this gift through long years of study, observation, and close application in any one of the ways in which fine art finds expression, is the training of the artist's brain and heart and hand. The better a human mind is trained to the perception of beauty the more opportunities will it find of exercising this precious gift, and the more directly will it be brought to bear upon even the very simplest matters of everyday life, and always to their bettering.

So it was in the wood of young seedling trees, where oak and holly, birch, beech and mountain ash, came up together in a close thicket of young saplings. It seemed well to consider, in the first place, how to bring something like order into the mixed jumble, and, the better to do this, to appeal to the little trees themselves and see what they had to say about it.

The ground runs on a natural slope downward to the north, or, to be more exact, as the highest point is at one corner, its surface is tilted diagonally all over. So, beginning at the lower end of the woody growth, near the place where the house some day might stand, the first thing that appeared was a well-grown holly, and rather near it, another ; both older trees than the more recent seedling growth. Close to the second holly was a young birch, the trunk about four inches thick and already in the early pride of its silvering bark. That was enough to prompt the decision that this part of the wood should be of silver birch and holly, so nearly all other growths were cut down or pulled up. A hundred yards higher up there were some strong young oaks, then some beeches, and all over the top of the ground a thick growth of young Scots pine, while the western region had a good sprinkling of promising Spanish chestnut.

All these natural groupings were accepted, and a first thinning was made of the smallest stuff of other kinds. But it was done with the most careful watching, for there were to be no harsh frontiers. One kind of tree was to join hands with the next, though often a distinct deviation was made to the general rule. For the beautiful growth of the

future wood was the thing that mattered, rather than obedience to any inflexible law.

Now, after twenty years, the saplings have become trees, and the preponderance of one kind of tree at a time has given a feeling of repose and dignity. Here and there something exceptional occurs, but it causes interest, not confusion. Five woodland walks pass upward through the trees; every one has its own character, while the details change during its progress – never abruptly, but in leisurely sequence; as if inviting the quiet stroller to stop a moment to enjoy some little woodland suavity, and then gently enticing him to go further, with agreeable anticipation of what might come next. And if I may judge by the pleasure that these woodland ways give to some of my friends who I know are in sympathy with what I am trying to do, and by my own thankful delight in them, I may take it that my little sylvan pictures have come fairly right, so that I may ask my reader to go with me in spirit through some of them.

My house, a big cottage, stands facing a little to the east of south, just below the wood. The windows of the sitting-room, and its outer door, which stands open in all fine summer weather, look up a straight wide grassy way, the vista being ended by a fine old Scots pine with a background of dark wood. This old pine and one other, and a number in and near the southern hedge, are all that remain of the older wood which was all of Scots pine.

This green wood walk, being the widest and most important, is treated more boldly than the others – with groups of rhododendrons in the region rather near the house, and for the rest only a biggish patch of the two North American brambles, the white-flowered *Rubus parviflorus*, and the rosy *R. odoratus*. In spring the western region of tall Spanish chestnuts, which begins just beyond the rhododendrons, is carpeted with poets' narcissus; the note of tender white blossom being taken up and repeated by the bloom-clouds of *Amelanchier*, that charming little woodland flowering tree whose use in such ways is so much neglected. Close to the ground in the distance the light comes with brilliant effect through the young leaves of a widespread carpet of lily of the valley, whose clusters of sweet little white bells will be a delight to see a month hence.

The rhododendrons are carefully grouped for colour – pink, white, rose and red of the best qualities are in the sunniest part, while, kept

This planting of pale narcissus, *Smilacina racemosa* (centre) and bronzy-leaved Rodgersia shows that Miss Jekyll's expansive drifts can be skilfully reduced to create a woodland atmosphere in the smallest garden.

well apart from them, near the tall chestnuts and rejoicing in their partial shade, are the purple colourings, of as pure and cool a purple as may be found among carefully selected *R. ponticum* seedlings and the few named kinds that associate well with them. Some details of this planting were given at length in my former book *Wood and Garden*.

Among the rhododendrons, at points carefully devised to be of good effect, either from the house or from various points of the lawn and grass paths, are strong groups of *Lilium auratum*; they give a new picture of flower-beauty in the late summer and autumn and till near the end of October. The dark, strong foliage makes the best possible setting for the lilies, and gives each group of them its fullest value. Another, narrower path, more to the east, is called the fern walk, because, besides the general growth of bracken that clothes the whole of the wood, there are groups of common hardy ferns in easy patches, planted in such a way as to suggest that they grew there naturally. The male fern, the beautiful dilated shield fern, and polypody are native to the ground, and it was easy to place these, in some cases merely adding to a naturally grown tuft, so that they look quite at home. Lady fern, *Blechnum* and *Osmunda*, and oak and beech ferns have been added, the osmunda in a depression that collects the water from any storms of rain. Later it was found that these wood-path edges offered suitable places for groups of the willow gentian (*G asclepiadea*), and it was rather largely planted. It delights in a cool place in shade or half-shade, and when in September so many flowers are over and garden plants in general are showing evidence of fatigue and exhaustion, it is a pleasant thing to come upon a group of the arching sprays of this graceful and quite distinctive plant with its bright blue flowers an inch and a half long set in pairs in the axils of the willow-like leaves.

At the beginning of all these paths I took some pains to make the garden melt imperceptibly into the wood, and in each case to do it a different way. Where this path begins the lawn ends at a group of oak, holly, and *Cistus*, with an undergrowth of *Gaultheria* and *Pieris*. The larger trees are to the left, and the small evergreen shrubs on a rocky mound to the right. Within a few yards the turf path becomes a true wood path. Just as wild gardening should never look like garden gardening, or, as it so sadly often does, like garden plants gone astray and quite out of place, so wood paths should never look like garden paths. There must be no hard edges, no obvious boundaries. The wood

32

The wide wood-path

path is merely an easy way that the eye just perceives and the foot follows. It dies away imperceptibly on either side into the floor of the wood and is of exactly the same nature, only that it is smooth and easy and is not encumbered by projecting tree-roots, bracken or bramble, these being all removed when the path is made.

If it is open enough to allow of the growth of grass, and the grass has to be cut, and is cut with a machine, then a man with a faghook must follow to cut away slantingly the hard edge of standing grass that is left on each side. For the track of the machine not only leaves the hard, unlovely edges, but also brings into the wood the incongruous sentiment of that discipline of trimness which belongs to the garden, and that, even there in its own place, is often overdone.

Now we are in the true wood path among oaks and birches. Looking round, the view is here and there stopped by prosperous-looking hollies, but for the most part one can see a fair way into the wood. In April the wood floor is plentifully furnished with daffodils. Here, in the region furthest removed from the white poets' daffodil of the upper ground, they are all of trumpet kinds, and the greater number of strong yellow colour. For the daffodils range through the wood in a

regular sequence of kinds that is not only the prettiest way to have them, but that I have often found, in the case of people who did not know their daffodils well, served to make the whole story of their general kinds and relationships clear and plain ; the hybrids of each group standing between the parent kinds ; these again leading through other hybrids to further clearly defined species, ending with the pure trumpets. As the sorts are intergrouped at their edges, so that at least two removes are in view at one time, the lesson in the general relationship of kinds is easily learnt.

Daffodils in drifts of separate kinds . . . . 'a singularly happy effect'. Fritillaries and other small bulbs can also be naturalized to extend the season.

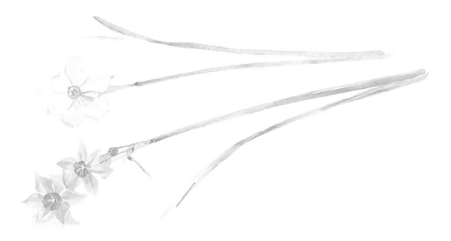

They are planted not in patches, but in long drifts, a way that not only shows the plant in good number to better advantage, but that is singularly happy in its effect in the woodland landscape. This is specially noticeable towards the close of the day, when the sunlight, yellowing as it nears the horizon, lights up the long stretches of yellow bloom with an increase of colour strength, while the wide-stretching shadow-lengths throw the woodland shades into large *phrases* of broadened mass, all subdued and harmonized by the same yellow light that illuminates the long level ranks of golden bloom.

From this same walk in June, looking westward through the birch stems, the value of the careful colour scheme of the rhododendrons is fully felt. They are about a hundred yards away, and their mass is broken by the groups of intervening tree-trunks ; but their brightness is all the more apparent seen from under the nearer roofing mass of tree-top, and the yellowing light makes the intended colour-effect still

The white Poets' daffodil and a small cupped narcissus 'of the Barrii kind'.

White foxgloves spire up to illuminate dark corners of the woodland garden. When seed was ripe Miss Jekyll scattered it in places where tree-stumps had been grubbed, to heal the scars.

more successful by throwing its warm tone over the whole.

But nearer at hand the fern walk has its own little pictures. In early summer there are patches of *Trillium*, the white wood lily, in cool hollows among the ferns, and, some twenty paces further up, another wider group of the same. Between the two, spreading through a mossy bank, in and out among the ferns and right down to the path, next to a coming patch of oak fern, is a charming little white flower. Its rambling roots thread their way under the mossy carpet, and every few inches throw up a neat little stem and leaves crowned with a starry flower of tenderest white. It is *Trientalis europaea*, a native of our most northern hill-woods, the daintiest of all woodland flowers.

To right and left white foxgloves spire up among the bracken. When the foxglove seed is ripe, we remember places in the wood where tree-stumps were grubbed last winter. A little of the seed is scattered in these places and raked in. Meanwhile one forgets all about it, till two years afterwards there are the stately foxgloves. It is good to see their strong spikes of solid bloom standing six to seven feet high, and then to look down again at the lowly *Trientalis* and to note how the tender little blossom, poised on its thread-like stem, holds its own in interest and importance.

Further up the fern walk, near the upper group of *Trillium*, are some patches of a plant with roundish, glittering leaves. It is a North American asarum *(A. virginianum)*; the curious wax-like brown and greenish flower, after the usual manner of its kind, is short-stalked and hidden at the base of the leaf-stems. Near it, and growing close to the ground in a tuft of dark-green moss, is an interesting plant – *Goodyera repens*, a terrestrial orchid. One might easily pass it by, for its curiously white-veined leaves are half hidden in the moss, and its spike of pale greenish-white flower is not conspicuous; but, knowing it is there, I never pass without kneeling down, both to admire its beauty and also to ensure its well-being by a careful removal of a little of the deep moss here and there where it threatens too close an invasion.

Now there comes a break in the fern walk, or rather it takes another character. The end of one of the wide green ways that we call the lily path comes into it on the right, and immediately beyond this, stands the second of the great Scots pines of the older wood. The trunk, at five feet from the ground, has a girth of nine and a half feet. The colour of the rugged bark is a wonder of lovely tones of cool greys and greens,

Bottom to top: Shield fern, *Maianthemum biflorum* and whortleberry (*Vaccinium myrtillus*).

and of a luminous deep brown in the fissures and cavities. Where the outer layers have flaked off it is a warm reddish grey, of a quality that is almost peculiar to itself. This great tree's storm-rent head towers up some seventy feet, far above the surrounding foliage of oak and birch. Close to its foot, and showing behind it as one comes up the fern walk, are a holly and a mountain ash.

This spot is a meeting-place of several ways. On the right the wide green of the lily path; then, still bearing diagonally to the right, one of the paths into the region of azalea and *Cistus*; then, straight past the big tree, a wood walk carpeted with whortleberry that passes through a whole whortleberry region under oaks, hollies and beeches; and, lastly, the path which is the continuation of the fern walk. Looking along it one sees, a little way ahead, a closer shade of trees, for the most part oak, but before entering this, on the right-hand gently rising bank, is a sheet of bright green leaves, closely set in May with neat spikes of white bloom. It is *Maianthemum bifolium*. The pretty little plant has taken to the place in a way that rejoices the heart of the wild gardener, joining in perfect accord with the natural growth of

38

short whortleberry and a background of the graceful fronds of dilated shield fern, and looking as if it was of spontaneous growth.

Now the path passes a large holly, laced through and through with wild honeysuckle. The honeysuckle stems that run up into the tree look like great ropes, and a quantity of the small ends come showering out of the tree-top and over the path, like a tangled veil of small cordage.

The path has been steadily rising, and now the ascent is a little steeper. The character of the trees is changing ; oaks are giving way to Scots pines. Just where this change begins, the bank to right and left is covered with the fresh, strong greenery of *Gaultheria shallon*. About twenty years ago a few small pieces were planted. Now it is a mass of close green growth two to three feet high and thirty paces long, and extending for several yards into the wood to right and left. In a light, peaty soil such as this, it is the best of undershrubs. It is in full leaf-beauty in the dead of winter, while in early summer it bears clusters of good flowers of the arbutus type. These are followed by handsome dark berries nearly as large as black currants, covered with a blue-grey bloom.

Now the path crosses another of the broad turfy ways, but here the turf is all of heath ; a fourteen-foot-wide road of grey-rosy bloom in August ; and now we are in the topmost region of Scots pine, with undergrowth of whortleberry.

The wood path next to this goes nearly straight up through the middle of the ground. It begins at another point of the small lawn next the house, and passes first by a turf walk through a mounded region of small shrubs and carefully placed pieces of the local sandstone. *Pieris, Skimmia* and alpenrose have grown into solid masses, so that the rocky ridges peer out only here and there. And when my friends say, 'But then, what a chance you had with that shelf of rock coming naturally out of the ground,' I feel the glowing warmth of an inward smile and think that perhaps the stones have not been so badly placed.

Near the middle of the woody ground a space was cleared that would be large enough to be sunny throughout the greater part of the day. This was for cistuses. It is one of the compensations for gardening on the poorest of soils that these delightful shrubs do well with only the preparation of digging up and loosening the sand, for my soil is nothing better. The kinds that are best in the woody landscape are

C. laurifolius and *C. × cyprius*; *C. laurifolius* is the hardiest, *C. × cyprius* rather the more beautiful, with its three-and-a-half-inch wide flowers of tenderest white with a red-purple blotch at the base of each petal. Its growth, also, is rather more free and graceful. *C. ladanifer* is similiar and flowers from July onwards. *C. laurifolius* is a bush of a denser habit; it bears an abundance of bloom rather smaller than that of *C. × cyprius*, and without the coloured blotch. But when it grows old and some of its stems are borne down and lie along the ground, the habit changes and it acquires a free pictorial character. These two large-growing cistuses are admirable for wild planting in sunny wood edges. They are used not only in their own ground, but by the sides of the grassy ways and the regions where the wood paths leave the lawn.

The sheltered, sunny cistus clearing has an undergrowth of wild heaths that are native to the ground, but a very few other heaths are added, namely, *Erica ciliata* and the Cornish heath; and there is a fine patch at the joining of two of the little grassy paths of the white form of the Irish heath (*Daboecia cantabrica*).

A project is in contemplation for a further extension of the clearing for the making of a heath garden, that promises to provide many happy hours of work in the coming winter.

Chapter III

THE SPRING GARDEN

As my garden falls naturally into various portions, distinct enough from each other to allow of separate treatment, I have found it well to devote one space at a time, sometimes mainly, sometimes entirely, to the flowers of one season of the year.

There is therefore one portion that is a complete little garden of spring flowers. It begins to show some bloom by the end of March, but its proper season is the month of April and three weeks of May.

In many places the spring garden has to give way to the summer garden, a plan that greatly restricts the choice of plants, and necessarily excludes some of the finest flowers of the early year.

My spring garden lies at the end and back of a high wall that shelters the big summer flower border from the north and north-west winds. The line of the wall is continued as a yew hedge that in time will rise to nearly the same height, about eleven feet. At the far end the yew hedge returns to the left so as to fence in the spring flowers from the east and to hide some sheds. The space also encloses some beds of tree peonies and a plot of grass, roughly circular in shape, about eight yards across, which is nearly surrounded by oaks, hollies and cob-nuts. It is of no design ; the space was accepted with its own conditions, arranged in the simplest way as to paths, and treated very carefully for colour. It really makes as pretty a picture of spring flowers as one could wish to see.

The chief mass of colour is in the main border. Gardens of spring flowers generally have a thin, poor effect for want of plants of important foliage. The greater number of them look what they are — temporary makeshifts. It seemed important that in this little space, which is given almost entirely to spring flowers, this weakness should not be allowed. But herbaceous plants of rather large growth with fine foliage in April and May are not many. The best I could think of are *Veratrum nigrum*, *Myrrhis odorata* and the newer *Euphorbia wulfenii*. The myrrhis is the sweet Cicely of old English gardens. It is an

Euphorbias were much admired by Miss Jekyll for their solid outlines, soft grey-green foliage and long-lasting flowers. Here the sharp yellow contrasts with English bluebells and introduces the warmer yellows and oranges of the azalea border.

umbelliferous plant with large fern-like foliage that makes early growth and flowers in the beginning of May. At three years old a well-grown plant is a yard high and across. After that, if the plants are not replaced by young ones, they grow too large, though they can be kept in check by a careful removal of the outer leaves and by cutting out some whole crowns when the plant is making its first growth. The veratrum, with its large, deeply plaited, undivided leaves, is in striking contrast, but the two kinds of plants, in groups, with running patches of the large form of *Bergenia cordifolia*, the great *Euphorbia wulfenii* and some groups of black hellebore, just give that comfortable impression of permanence and distinct intention that are usually so lamentably absent from gardens of spring flowers.

Many years ago I came to the conclusion that in all flower borders it is better to plant in long rather than block-shaped patches. It not only has a more pictorial effect, but a thin long planting does not leave an unsightly empty space when the flowers are done and the leaves have perhaps died down. The word 'drift' conveniently describes the shape I have in mind, and I commonly use it in speaking of these long-shaped plantings.

There are of course many plants that look best in a distinct clump or even as single examples, such as *Dictamnus* (the burning bush), and the beautiful pale yellow *Paeonia wittmanniana*, a single plant of which is near the beginning of the main border.

For the first seven or eight yards, in the front and middle spaces, there are plants of tender colouring – pale primroses, *Tiarella*, pale yellow daffodils, pale yellow early iris, pale lemon wallflower, double *Arabis*, white anemones and the palest of the lilac aubrietas; also a beautiful pale lilac iris, one of the Intermediate hybrids; with long drifts of white and pale yellow tulips – nothing deeper in colour than the graceful *Tulipa retroflexa*. At the back of the border the colours are darker; purple wallflower and the great dull red-purple double tulip so absurdly called 'Bleu Celeste'. These run through and among and be-hind the first clump of veratrums.

In the middle of the length of the border there is still a good proportion of tender and light colouring in front: white primroses and daffodils; the pale yellow *Uvularia* and *Adonis vernalis*; but with these there are stronger colours: *Tulipa* 'Chrysolora' of fuller yellow, yellow wallflowers, the tall *Doronicum*, and, towards the back, several patches

Top to bottom: *Tiarella cordifolia*, pale yellow early iris and the 'palest of the lilac aubrietas'.

of yellow crown imperial.

Then again in front, with more double *Arabis*, is the lovely pale blue of *Myosotis dissitiflora* and *Mertensia virginica*, and, with sheets of the foam-like *Tiarella*, the tender pink of *Dicentra eximia* and pink and rose-red tulips. At the back of this come scarlet tulips, the stately cream-white form of *Camassia leichtlinii* and a bold tuft of Solomon's seal; then orange tulips, brown wallflowers, orange crown imperial, and taller scarlet varieties of *Tulipa gesneriana*. The strong colouring is repeated beyond the cross-path near the patches of *Acanthus*, with more orange tulips, brown wallflowers, orange crown imperial and great flaming scarlet gesneriana tulips. All this shows up finely against the background of dark yew. At the extreme end, where the yew hedge returns forward at a right angle, this point is accentuated by a raised mound of triangular shape, dry-walled and siightly curved forward on the side facing the border and the spectator. On this at the back is a young plant of *Yucca gloriosa* for display in future years and a front planting of the large-growing *Euphorbia wulfenii*, one of the grandest and most pictorial of plants of recent acquirement for garden use.

Acanthus and *Yucca* are of course plants of middle and late summer; between them are some kniphofias. These plants are here because one

44

of the most often used of the garden thoroughfares passes beneath a thick-roofed arch of rose and clematis, and, seen from this point and framed by the near greenery, they form a striking picture of middle-distant form and colour in the later summer.

To the left of this is an upward-sloping bank, with a big piece of sandstone that looks as if it came naturally out of the ground, and with hollies standing on rather higher ground. Here the plants are between, and tumbling over, rocky ridges. Next the large holly, and extending to the middle of the rocky promontory, are again the strong reds and browns, with accompanying bronze-red foliage of *Heuchera hispida*. This gives place to dark green carpeting masses of *Iberis* with cold-white bloom, and, nearer the path, *Lithospermum diffusum* ; the flower-colour here changing, through white, to blue and bluish ; *Myosotis* in front telling charmingly against the dark-leaved lithospermum. At the highest points, next to a great crowning boulder, is the common blue iris and a paler one of the beautiful Intermediate series. Then down to the path where it begins to turn is a drift of the bluish-lilac *Phlox divaricata*, and, opposite the cross-path, some jewels of the newer pale yellow *Alyssum saxatile* var. *citrinum*. This rocky shoulder is also enlivened by a natural-looking but very carefully considered planting of white tulips that run through both the blue and the red regions. A view towards this bank from the west shows the value of the dark yew hedge as a background to the flowers. Just at the back of the flowery bank are hollies, and then the hedge. This has not yet come to its full height and the top still shows a ragged outline, but in two years' time it will have grown into shape.

The corner near the rose and clematis arch is also a slightly raised bank. Garlands of *Clematis montana* swing on ropes between cob-nuts. The garlands dip down and nearly meet the flowers of some pale pink tree peonies. Open spaces above the garlands and under the meeting branches of the nuts give glimpses of distant points where some little scheme has been devised to please the eye, such as the bit of bank to the left of a seat where there are two little fish-like drifts of palest *Aubrieta* in a dense grey setting of *Cerastium*.

The corner next the path agrees with the colouring opposite, but also has features of its own ; a groundwork of grey *Antennaria*, the soft lilac-pink of the good *Aubrieta deltoidea* 'Moerheimii' changing to the left to the fuller pink of *Phlox amœna*, and above to the type colour of

45

aubrieta and some of the strong purples such as the variety 'Dr Mules'. To the left, towards the oaks, the colouring is mostly purple, with stout tufts of the spring bitter vetch *(Lathyrus vernus)*, purple wallflowers, and, under and behind the nuts, purple honesty. Thin streams of white tulips intermingle with other streams of pink tulips that crown the angle and flow down again to the main path between ridges of double *Arabis*, white *Iberis*, and cloudy masses of the pretty pale yellow *Corydalis ochroleuca*, which spreads into a wide carpet under the tree peonies and clematis garlands.

Further along, just clear of the nuts, are some patches of *Dicentra spectabilis*, its graceful growth arching out over the lower stature of pink tulips and harmonizing charmingly with the pinkish-green foliage of the tree peonies just behind. The pink tulips are here in some quantity ; they run boldly into pools of pale blue *Myosotis*, with more *Iberis* where the picture demands the strongest, deepest green, and more *Corydalis* where the softer, greyer tones will make it better.

The space that is always in shade from the nuts and oaks is planted with rather large patches of the handsome white-flowered *Dentaria*, the graceful North American *Uvularia grandiflora*, in habit like a small Solomon's seal, but with yellow flowers much larger in proportion ;

Thin streams of white and pink tulips over cloudy masses of pale blue forget-me-not epitomize the delicate brilliance of the spring garden. Pheasant-eye narcissus provide a brighter sparkle among the tulips.

Aubrieta, *Phlox amoena* and white and pink tulips in the Spring garden.

with *Myrrhis* and purple honesty at the back and sheets of sweet woodruff to the front.

There are tree peonies in the long border and the two others. It is difficult to grow them in my hot, dry, sandy soil, even though I make them a liberal provision of just such a compost as I think they will like. I have noticed that they do best when closely overshadowed by some other growing thing. In the two near beds there are some 'Mme Alfred Carrière' roses that are trained to arch over to the angles, so as to comfort and encourage the peonies. These beds have an informal edging of *Stachys lanata*, one of the most useful of plants for grey effects. Through it come white tulips in irregular patches.

The long border has also tree peonies planted about two and a half feet from the edge. Partly to give the bed a sort of backbone, and partly to shelter the tree peonies, it has some bushes of *Hebe brachysiphon* and one or two *Leycesteria formosa*. In the middle of the length is a clump of *Cardiocrinum giganteum* and a biggish grouping of *Dicentra spectabilis*. All along the outer border there are patches and long straggling groups of the pretty dwarf irises of the pumila, olbiensis and chamæ-iris sections, with others of the same class of stature and habit. Any bare spaces are filled with wallflowers and honesty in colours that accord with the general arrangement. The narrow border has mostly small shrubs, *Berberis* and so on, forming one mass with the hedge to the left, which consists of a double dry wall about four feet high, with earth between and a thick growth on the top of *Berberis*, *Rosa virginiana* and Burnet roses. Except the *Berberis* these make no show of flower within the blooming time of the spring garden, but the whole is excellent as a background.

Red primroses are in the narrow border next to the cross-wall; the wall here is much lower than the longer one on the right. The primroses are grouped with the reddish-leaved *Heuchera hispida*, the two together making a rich colour-harmony. Beyond them are scarlet tulips. In this border and continuing across the path into the near end of the main border are stout larch posts supporting a strong growth of *Rosa* 'Mme Alfred Carrière' and *Clematis montana*. These plants have grown together into a solid continuously intermingling mass, the path passing under a low arch of their united branches. The high wall on the right is also covered with flowering things of the early year, morello cherries, *Rubus deliciosus* and *Clematis montana*, some of this

Top: *Heuchera hispida*;
bottom: red primroses.

foaming over from the other side of the wall.

The wall is a part, about a third of the length, of the high wall that protects the large border of summer and autumn flowers from the north, and that forms the dividing-line between the pleasure garden proper and the working garden beyond.

The view of the garden from the rose and clematis arch shows two-thirds of the longest path with the end of the big wall and the yew hedge that prolongs its line on the right and the nut-trees on the left. The colouring on the right is of pale purple aubrieta and double white arabis, with pale daffodils, and, at the back, groups of sulphur crown imperial. The more distant colouring is of brown wallflower and red tulip and the bright mahogany-coloured crown imperial. The view eastwards from among the reds and strong yellows looks through the arch of rose and clematis, to the summer garden beyond.

The primrose garden is in a separate place among oaks and hazels. It is for my special strain of large yellow and white bunch primroses, now arrived at a state of fine quality and development by a system of careful seed-selection that has been carried on for more than thirty years.

Chapter IV

BETWEEN SPRING
AND SUMMER

WHEN the spring flowers are done, and before the full June days come with the great flag irises and the perennial lupins, there is a kind of mid-season. If it can be given a space of ground it will be well bestowed. I have a place that I call the Hidden Garden, because it is in a corner that might so easily be overlooked if one did not know where to find it. No important path leads into it, though two pass within ten yards of it on either side. It is in a sort of clearing among *Quercus ilex* and holly, and the three small ways into it are devious and scarcely noticeable from the outside. The most important of these passes between some clumps of over-arching bamboo and through a short curved tunnel of yew and *Quercus ilex*. Another is only just traceable among *Berberis* under a large birch, and comes sharply round a tall Monterey cypress. The third turns out of one of the shady woodland glades and comes into the little garden by some rough stone steps.

The arrangement is simple, the paths following the most natural lines that the place suggests. The main path goes down some shallow, rough stone steps with a sunny bank to the left and a rocky mound to the right. The mound is crowned with small shrubs, alpine rhododendrons and *Pieris*. Both this and the left-hand bank have a few courses of rough dry-walling next the path on its lowest level. A little cross-path curves into the main one from the right.

The path leaves the garden again by a repetition of the rough stone steps. The mossy growth of *Arenaria balearica* clings closely to the stones on their cooler faces, and the frond-like growths of Solomon's seal hang out on either side as a fitting prelude to the dim mysteries of the wide green wood path beyond.

It is a garden for the last days of May and the first fortnight of June. Passing through the yew tunnel, the little place bursts on the sight with good effect. What is most striking is the beauty of the blue-lilac *Phlox divaricata* and that of two clumps of tree peony[3] – the rosy 'Elizabeth' and the pale salmon-pink 'Comtesse de Tuder'. The little garden, with its quiet environment of dark foliage, forbids the use of strong colouring, or perhaps one should say that it suggested a restriction of the scheme of colouring to the tenderer tones. There seemed to be no place here for the gorgeous oriental poppies, although they too are finest in partial shade, or for any strong yellows, their character needing wider spaces and clearer sunlight.

The tree peonies are in two groups of the two kinds only; it seemed enough for the limited space. In front of 'Comtesse de Tuder' is a group of *Hosta sieboldiana*, its bluish leaves harmonizing delightfully with the leaf-colour of the peonies; next to them is a corner of glistening deep green *Asarum*. No other flowers of any size are near, but there are sheets of the tender yellow bloom and pale foliage of *Corydalis ochroleuca*, of the white-bloomed woodruff, and the pale green leafage of *Epimedium*; and among them tufts of Lent hellebores, also in fresh young leaf, and a backing of the feathery fronds of lady fern and of the

Top to bottom: Tree peony, *Hosta sieboldiana* and *Asarum europaeum*.

Top right to bottom: Corydalis ochroleuca, Solomon's seal and epimedium.

large Solomon's seal; with drooping garlands of *Clematis montana* hanging informally from some rough branching posts. Yew-trees are at the back, and then beeches in tender young leaf.

The foot of the near mound is a pink cloud of London pride. Shooting up among it and just beyond is the white St Bruno's lily. More of this lovely little lily-like *Anthericum* is again a few feet further along, grouped with *Iris cengialti*[4], one of the bluest of the irises. The back of the mound has some of the tenderly tinted Intermediate hybrid irises two feet high, of pale lilac colouring, rising from among dark-leaved, white-bloomed iberis, and next the path a pretty, large-flowered tufted pansy that nearly matches the iris.

But the glory of the mound is the long stretch of blue-lilac *Phlox divaricata*, whose colour is again repeated by a little of the same on the sunny bank to the left. Here it is grouped with pale pink Scotch brier, more pale yellow *Corydalis* and *Arenaria montana* smothered in its masses of white bloom. At the end of the bank the colour of the *Phlox divaricata* is deepened by sheaves of *Camassia quamash* that spear up through it. The whole back of this bank has a free planting of graceful pale-coloured columbines with long spurs, garden kinds that come

52

easily from seed and that were originally derived from some North American species. They are pale yellow and warm white; some have the outer portion of the flower of a faint purple, much like that of some of the patches in an old, much-washed, cotton patchwork quilt.

The dark trees on the right have rambling roses growing into them – 'Paul's Carmine Pillar' and the Himalayan *R. brunonii*. The red rose does not flower so freely here as on a pillar in sunlight, but its fewer stems clamber high into the holly, and the bloom shows in thin natural wreaths that are even more pleasing to an artist's eye than the more ordered abundance of the flowery post. At the foot of the hollies hardy ferns grow luxuriantly in the constant shade. A little later a few clumps of lilies will spring up from among them; the lovely pink *Lilium rubellum*, the fine yellow *L. szovitsianum*, and the buff *L. × testaceum*.

On the left-hand side, behind the sunny bank, a 'Garland' rose comes through and tumbles out of a yew, and some sprays of an old bush of the single *R. multiflora*, that has spread to a circumference of one hundred and fifty feet, have pushed their way through the *Quercus ilex*.

The hollies and *Quercus ilex* all round are growing fast, and before many years are over the little garden will become too shady for the well-being of the flowers that now occupy it. It will then change its character and become a fern garden.

All gardening involves constant change. It is even more so in woodland. A young bit of wood such as mine is for ever changing. Happily, each new development reveals new beauty of aspect or new possibility of good treatment, such as, rightly apprehended and then guided, tends to a better state than before.

Meanwhile the little tree-embowered garden has a quiet charm of its own. It seems to delight in its character of a Hidden Garden, and in the pleasant surprise that its sudden discovery provokes. For between it and its owner there is always a pretty little play of pretending that there is no garden there, and of being much surprised and delighted at finding, not only that there is one, but quite a pretty one.

The Hidden Garden is so small in extent, and its boundaries are already so well grown, that there is no room for many of the beautiful things of the time of year. For May is the time for the blooming of the most important of our well-known flowering shrubs – lilac, guelder rose, white broom, laburnum, and *Malus floribunda*. But one shrub, as

53

beautiful as any of these and as easily grown, seems to be forgotten. This is *Exochorda racemosa* – related to the spiraeas. Its pearl-like buds have earned it the name of pearl bush, but its whole lovely bloom should before now have secured it a place in every good garden.

Every one knows the guelder rose, with its round white flower-balls, but the wild shrub of which this is a garden variety is also a valuable ornamental bush and should not be neglected. It is a native plant, growing in damp places, such as the hedges of water-meadows and the sides of streams. The English name is water elder. Its merit as a garden shrub does not lie, as in the guelder rose, in its bloom, but in its singularly beautiful fruit. This, in autumn, lights up the whole shrub with a ruddy radiance. Grown on drier ground than that of its natural habitat, it takes a closer, more compact form.

White broom is in flower from the middle of May to the second week of June. There is a fine flag iris of a rich purple colour called 'Purple King'. It is well to grow it just in front of some young bushes of white broom. Then, if one of the hybrid irises of pale lilac colour is there as well, and a bush of *Rosa pimpinellifolia* var. *altaica*, the colour-effect will be surprisingly beautiful. This rose is the bolder-growing, Asiatic equivalent of our Burnet rose, with the same lemon-white

Climbing roses (here *Rosa* 'Kiftsgate') cascading through holly created, for Miss Jekyll, one of the most satisfying of garden pictures. Fleeting white flowers among dark evergreen foliage and arching swags against the stiff upright branches of holly provide contrasts of the most telling kind.

Left: The pearl bush, *Exochorda racemosa*; right: white broom (*Cytisus albus*).

55

The white flowers of *Rubus × tridel* (left) and feathery lilacs shed light into a dark corner of the garden with sturdy iris continuing the theme at a lower level. Even a solitary tulip flower contributes to the effect.

Plan of the Hidden garden

flowers. When any such group containing white broom is planted, it should be remembered that the tendency of the broom is to grow tall and leggy. It bears pruning, but it is a good plan to plant some extra ones behind the others. After a couple of years, if the front plants have grown out of bounds, the back ones can be bent down and fastened to sticks, so that their heads come in the required places. It is one of the many ways in which a pretty garden picture may be maintained from year to year by the exercise of a little thought and ingenuity. The undergrowth of such a group may be of Solomon's seal at the back, and, if the bank or border is in sun, of a lower groundwork of *Iberis* and *Corydalis ochroleuca*, or, if it is shaded, of *Tiarella*, woodruff or *Anemone sylvestris*. With these, for the sake of their tender green foliage, there may well be *Uvularia grandiflora* and *Epimedium pinnatum*. There is now a dwarf form of the white broom, a plant not only less in height but of a more close and compact shape, that is useful for grouping in front of the older, taller one as well as for use in places where the original plant is too large.

A wonderful plant of May is the great *Euphorbia wulfenii*. It adapts itself to many ways of use, for, though the immense yellow-green heads of bloom are at their best in May, they are still of pictorial value

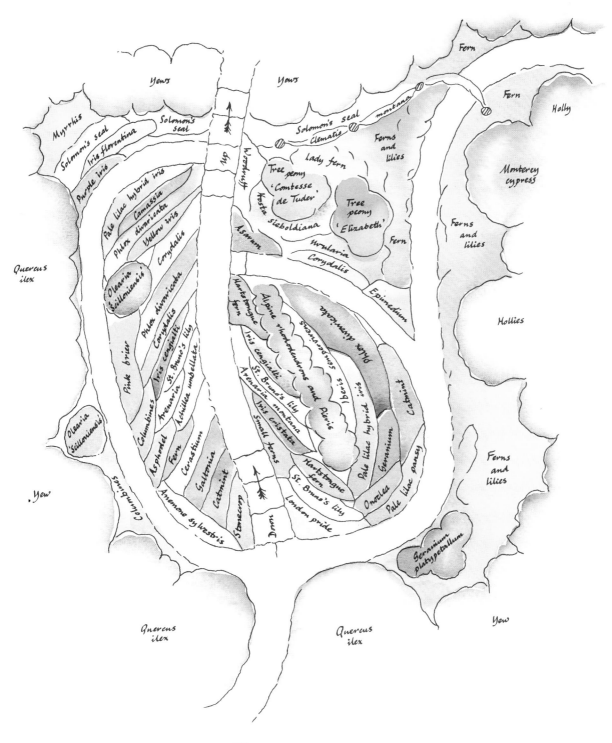

in June and July, while the deep-toned, grey-blue foliage is in full beauty throughout the greater part of the year. It is valuable in boldly arranged flower borders, and holds its own among shrubs of moderate size, but I always think its best use would be in the boldest kind of rock-work.

One of my desires that can never be fulfilled is to have a rocky hill-side in full sun, so steep as to be almost precipitous, with walls of bare rock only broken by ledges that can be planted. I would have great groups of *Yucca* standing up against the sky and others in the rock-face, and some bushes of this great euphorbia and only a few other plants, all of rather large grey effect; Phlomis, lavender, rosemary and *Cistus*, with *Othonnopsis cheirifolia* hanging down in long sheets over the bare face of the warm rock. It would be a rock-garden on an immense scale, planted as Nature plants, with not many different things at a time. The restriction to a few kinds of plants would give the impression of spontaneous growth; of that large, free, natural effect that is so rarely achieved in artificial planting. Besides natural hill-sides, there must be old quarries within or near the pleasure-grounds of many places in our islands where such a scheme of planting could worthily be carried out.

Chapter V

THE JUNE GARDEN

BEYOND the lawn and a belt of Spanish chestnut I have a little cottage that is known as the Hut. I lived in it for two years while my house was building, and may possibly live in it again for the sake of replenishing an over-drained exchequer, if the ideal well-to-do invalid flower-lover or some such very quiet summer tenant, to whom alone I could consent to surrender my dear home for a few weeks, should be presented by kind Providence. Meanwhile it is always in good use for various purposes, such as seed-drying, *pot-pourri* preparing, and the like.

The garden in front and at the back is mainly a June garden. It has peonies, irises, lupins, and others of the best flowers of the season, and a few for later blooming. The entrance to the Hut is through yews that arch overhead. Close to the right is a tall holly with a *Clematis montana* growing into it and tumbling out at the top. The space of garden to the left, being of too deep a shape to be easily got at from the path on the one side and the stone paving on the other, has a kind of dividing backbone made of a double row of rose hoops or low arches, rising from good greenery of male fern and the fern-like sweet Cicely. This handsome plant (*Myrrhis odorata*) is of great use in many ways. It will grow anywhere, and has the unusual merit of making a good show of foliage quite early in the year. It takes two years to get to a good size, sending its large, fleshy, aromatic roots deep down into the soil. By the end of May, when the bloom is over and the leaves are full grown, they can be cut right down, when the plant will at once form a new set of leaves that remain fresh for the rest of the summer. Its chief use is as a good foliage accompaniment or background to flowers, and no plant is better for filling up at the bases of shrubs that look a little leggy near the ground, or for any furnishing of waste or empty spaces, especially in shade. From among the ferns and *Myrrhis* at the back of this bit of eastern border rise white foxgloves, the great white columbine, and the tall stems of white peach-leaved campanula (*Campanula persicifolia*). Nearer to the front are clumps of peonies. But as one of the most frequented paths passes along this eastern border, it was thought best not to confine it to June flowers only, but to have something also for the later months. All vacant places are therefore filled with penstemons and snapdragons, which make a show thoughout the summer ; while for the early days of July there are clumps of the old garden roses – Damask and Provence. The whole south-western angle is occupied by a well-grown 'Garland' rose that every summer is loaded with its graceful wreaths of bloom. It has never been trained or staked, but grows as a natural fountain ; the branches are neither pruned nor shortened. The only attention it receives is that every three or four years the internal mass of old dead wood is cut right out, when the bush seems to spring into new life.

Passing this angle and going along the path leading to the studio door in the little stone-paved court, there is a seat under an arbour formed by the yews ; the front of it has a rambler rose, 'Sanders' White Rambler', supported by a rough wooden framework. On the right, next the paving, are two large standard roses with heads three and four feet through. They are old garden roses, worked in cottage fashion on a common dog-rose stock. One is 'Céleste', of loveliest tender rose

Dusky pink roses, towering foxgloves, warm-white peonies and silver-leaved pear create a softness characteristic of Miss Jekyll's more subdued colour schemes. White lilies (*Lilium auratum*), supported by the peony foliage, and deep blue ceratostigma (foreground) will provide a brighter harmony with the pear later in the season.

Top right to bottom: The fern-like sweet Cicely (*Myrrhis odorata*), white foxglove and the greenery of male fern.

colour, its broad bluish leaves showing its near relationship to *Rosa alba*; the other the white 'Mme Plantier'. This old rose, with its abundant bunches of pure white flowers, always seems to me to be one of the most charming of the older garden kinds. It will grow in almost any way, and is delightful in all; as a pillar, as a hedge, as a bush, as a big cottage standard, or in the border tumbling about among early summer flowers. Like the 'Blush Damask', which just precedes it in time of blooming, it is one of the old picture roses. Both should be in quantity in every garden, and yet they are but rarely to be seen.

The border next the paving has clumps of the old garden peonies (*Paeonia officinalis*). By the time these are over, towards the end of June, groups of the earlier orange herring lilies are in bloom. A thick and rather high box edging neatly trims these borders, and favours the cottage-garden sentiment that is fostered in this region. At the back of the yews that form the arbour is one end of the Hidden Garden. Going along the path, past the projection on the block-plan of the Hut, which represents the large ingle of the studio, we come to the other bit of June garden behind the little cottage. Here again, the space being over-wide, it is divided in the middle by a double border of rosemary that is kept clipped and is not allowed to rise high enough to prevent access to the border on each side.

On the side next the Hut the flowers are mostly of lilac and purple colouring with white. Pale lilac irises, including the fine *I. pallida* var. *dalmatica* and the rosy-lilac variety, 'Queen of the May'; perennial lupins, white, bluish lilac and purple – one of a conspicuous and rare deep red-purple of extreme richness without the slightest taint of a rank quality – a colour I can only call a strong wine-purple; then a clump of the feathery, ivory-white *Aruncus sylvester*, the large meadowsweet that is so fine by the side of alpine torrents. There are also some flesh-pink albiflora peonies and lower growths of catmint, and of the grand blue-purple cranesbill, *Geranium platypetalum*, with white and pale yellow Spanish irises in generous tufts springing up between. At the blunt angle nearly opposite the dovecote is a pink cloud of London pride; beyond it pale yellow violas with more white Spanish iris, leading to a happy combination of the blue *Iris cengialti* and the bushy aster *Olearia* 'Scilloniensis', smothered in its white starry bloom. An early flowering flag iris, named 'Chamæleon', nearly matches the colour of *I. cengialti*; it is the bluest that I know of the flag

irises, and is planted between and around the olearias to form part of the colour-picture.

Beyond this group, and only separated from it by some pale yellow irises, are two plants of the Dropmore *Anchusa* 'Opal' of pure pale blue, and another clump of *Aruncus sylvester* and one of a good pure white lupin, with some tall clear yellow irises and white foxgloves. Now the colouring changes, passing through a group or two of the rich half-tones of forms of *Iris squalens* to the perennial poppies – *Papaver rupifragum* nearest the path and, next to it, *P. pilosum* : both of a rich apricot colour. Backing these is a group of the larger hybrid that nearly always occurs in gardens where there are both *P. rupifragum* and *P. orientale*. In appearance it is a small *P. orientale* with a strong look of *P. rupifragum* about the foliage. As a garden plant it has the advantages of being of an intermediate size and of having a long season of bloom, a quality no doubt inherited from *P. rupifragum*, which will flower more or less throughout the summer if the seed-pods are removed. A plant of oriental poppy of the tone of orange-scarlet that I know as red-lead colour, and some deep orange lilies complete this strongly coloured group.

Top to bottom: Flesh-pink albiflora peony, *Geranium platypetalum* and catmint.

63

This is a scene of
harmony and contrast:
the soft tints of old
roses, apricot foxgloves,
peach-leaved campanula,
Iris spuria and the grey
foliage of santolina and
Achillea 'Moonshine' are
accentuated by the sharp
yellow of the achillea's
flowers.

In the north-western clump, where there are some thorn-trees and two thuyas, the dominant feature is the great bush of an old garden rambling rose that looks as if its parentage was somewhere between *Rosa sempervirens* and *R. arvensis*. I can neither remember how I came by it nor match it with any nursery kind. It stands nearly opposite the Hut kitchen window, and when in full bloom actually sheds light into the room. I know it as the kitchen rose. The diameter of the bush is even greater than the plan shows, for it overwhelms the nearest thuya and rushes through the thorn, and many of its shoots are within hand-reach of the back path. The rest of this clump is occupied by plants of tall habit – the great mullein (*Verbascum chaixii*), the giant cow-parsley (*Heracleum mantegazzianum*), and white foxgloves.

The border of early bulbs, described in a former chapter (now a mass of hardy ferns), lies farther to the west beyond this part of the garden. There is also a grand mass of oriental poppy and orange lilies (*Lilium bulbiferum* var. *croceum*) in half-shade on the other side of the path, where it turns and is bordered with *Berberis*. This makes a fine distant effect of strong colour looking north-west from the southern end of the bulb-border.

I greatly wish I could have some other June borders for the still better use of the flag irises, but not only have I quite as much dressed ground as I can afford to keep up, but the only space where such borders could be made has to be nursery-ground of plants for sale. But though I am denied this pleasure myself, I should like to suggest it to others. There would be no great harm if two borders of different colourings came opposite each other, though perhaps, as colour schemes, they would be rather better seen singly and quite detached from each other.

The first scheme of colouring would be of white, lilac, purple and pink, with grey foliage; the second of white, yellow, bronze-yellow and, for the most part, rich green foliage. They would show mainly as iris and lupin borders, and would be intended to display the beauty of these two grand plants of early summer. The kinds of iris would be carefully considered for their height, time of blooming and colour value. In the yellow border I should include one patch of clear, pale blue, the Dropmore *Anchusa* 'Opal', grouped with pale yellows and white.

It must be remembered, as in all cases of planting flower borders,

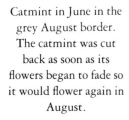

Catmint in June in the grey August border. The catmint was cut back as soon as its flowers began to fade so it would flower again in August.

that they cannot be expected to show their full beauty the year after planting. Irises will give a few blooms the first season, but are not in strength till their second and third years. China roses must have time to grow. Tree lupins must be planted young, and though they make rapid growth, they also do not fill their spaces till the third year. Their best colour is a clear, lively light yellow, but it readily varies from seed to whitish or washy purplish tints. As the seedlings often show bloom the first season in the seed-bed, the colours should be noted and marked, for some of the light purples are pretty things, with more refinement of character than the same colourings in the old tree lupins. Both the tree and hybrid kinds may have their lives much prolonged – for if they are not specially treated they are short-lived things – by judicious pruning. After flowering, each branch should be cut well back. It is not enough to cut away the flowers, but every branch should be shortened about two-thirds as soon as the bloom is over and the seed-pods begin to form.

In the purple border are some important front-edge patches of the beautiful catmint (*Nepeta mussinii*), a plant that can hardly be over-praised. For a good three weeks in June it makes this border a pretty place, although the catmint is its only flower. But with the white-grey woolly patches of *Stachys* and the half-grown bushes of *Gypsophila*, and the lavender and other plants of greyish foliage, the picture is by no means incomplete. Its flowery masses, seen against the warm yellow of the sandy path, give the impression of remarkably strong and yet delightfully soft colouring. The colour itself is a midway purple, between light and dark, of just the most pleasing quality. As soon as the best of the bloom is done it is carefully cut over; then the lateral shoots just below the main flower-spike that has been taken out will gain strength and bloom again at the border's best show-time in August. In another double flower border that is mostly for the September-blooming Michaelmas daisies the catmint is cut back a little later.

One of the joys of June is the beauty of the Burnet roses. On the south side of the house there are figs and vines, rosemary and China roses, and then a path, from which easy stone steps lead up to the strip of lawn some fifty feet wide that skirts the wood. To right and left of the steps, for a length equal to that of the house-front, is a hedge of these charming little roses. They are mostly double white, but some are rosy and some yellow. When it is not in flower the mass of small foliage is pleasant to see, and even in winter leaflessness the tangle of close-locked branches has an appearance of warm brown comfort that makes it good to have near a house.

June is also the time of some of the best of the climbing plants and slightly tender shrubs that we have against walls and treat as climbers, such as *Solanum crispum* and *Abutilon vitifolium* and the hardy *Clematis montana*; but some notes on these will be offered in a further chapter.

One is always watching and trying for good combinations of colour that occur or that may be composed. Besides such as are shown in the plans, the following have been noted for June:

In rock-work the China rose 'Natalie Nypels', also the tender pink 'Laurette Messimy', with pale lilac tufted pansy and *Achillea umbellata*.

The pretty pale pink dwarf rose 'Cameo', with the lilac of catmint (*Nepeta mussinii*) and the grey-white foliage of *Stachys* and *Senecio cineraria*.

In a cool, retired place in a shrubbery margin, away from other flowers, the misty red-grey-purple of *Thalictrum aquilegifolium* var. *atropurpureum* with the warm white foam-colour of *Aruncus sylvester*.

67

Above: Valerian (*Centranthus*); below: a deep scarlet-crimson snapdragon.

On bold rock-work, a mass of a fine-coloured strain of valerian (*Centranthus*) with a deep scarlet-crimson snapdragon. This is a success of reciprocally enhancing texture as well as colour; the texture having that satisfying quality that one recognizes in the relation of the cut and uncut portions of the fine old Italian cut-velvets.

In April *Narcissus jonquilla* with *Myosotis dissitiflora*.

In May the true blue *Pulmonaria angustifolia* 'Azurea' with the white form of *Scilla italica*.

In a shrubbery edge, or some cool, half shady place, the purple form of *Thalictrum aquilegifolium* with white foxgloves, and in the same kind of place *Campanula latifolia* var. *alba* and the fine purple *C. latiloba* with male fern or lady fern.

In an open, sunny place *Eryngium giganteum* with sea-kale.

In a section of flower border given to purple flowers *Salvia sclarea* with *S. nemorosa*, and purple-leaved sage at the foot.

Chapter VI

THE MAIN HARDY
FLOWER BORDER

THE big flower border is about two hundred feet long and fourteen feet wide. It is sheltered from the north by a solid sandstone wall about eleven feet high clothed for the most part with evergreen shrubs – bay and laurustinus, *Choisya*, *Cistus* and loquat. These show as a handsome background to the flowering plants. They are in a three-foot-wide border at the foot of the wall ; then there is a narrow alley, not seen from the front, but convenient for access to the wall shrubs and for working the back of the border.

As it is impossible to keep any one flower border fully dressed for the whole summer, and as it suits me that it should be at its best in the late summer, there is no attempt to have it full of flowers as early as June. Another region belongs to June ; so that at that time the big border has only some incidents of good bloom, though the ground is rapidly covering with the strong patches, most of them from three to five years old, of the later-blooming perennials. But early in the month there are some clumps of the beautiful *Iris pallida* var. *dalmatica* in the regions of grey foliage, and of the splendid blue-purple bloom of *Geranium platypetalum*, the best of the large cranesbills[5], and the slow-growing *Dictamnus albus* and meadowsweets white and pink, foxgloves and Canterbury bells, and to the front some long-established sheets of *Iberis sempervirens* that have grown right on to the path. The large *Yucca gloriosa* and *Y. recurvifolia* are throwing up their massive spikes, though it will be July before they actually flower, and the blooms on some bushes of the great *Euphorbia wulfenii*, although they were flowers of May and their almost yellow colour is turning greener, are still conspicuous and ornamental. Then the plants in the middle of the wall, *Choisya ternata* and *Clematis montana* are still full of white bloom, and the guelder rose is hanging out its great white balls. I like to plant the guelder rose and *Clematis montana* together. Nothing does better on

69

Clematis montana
and (below) the double
guelder rose.

north or east walls, and it is pleasant to see the way the clematis flings its graceful garlands over and through the stiff branches of the viburnum.

The more brilliant patches of colour in the big border in June are of oriental poppies intergrouped with *Gypsophila*, which will cover their space when they have died down, and the earlier forms of *Lilium bulbiferum croceum* of that dark orange colour that almost approaches scarlet.

During the first week of June any bare spaces of the border are filled up with half-hardy annuals, and some of what we are accustomed to call bedding-plants – such as *Pelargonium, Salvia, Calceolaria, Begonia, Gazania* and *Verbena*. The half-hardy annuals are African marigold, deep orange and pale sulphur, pure white single *Petunia*, tall *Ageratum*, tall striped maize, white cosmos, sulphur sunflower, *Phlox drummondii*, nasturtiums and *Trachelium cœruleum*. Dahlias were planted out in May, and earlier still the hollyhocks, quite young plants that are to bloom in August and September; the autumn-planted ones flowering earlier. The ground was well cleared of weeds before these were planted, and, soon after, the whole border had a good mulch of a mixture of half-rotted leaves and old hot-bed stuff. This serves the

The cross walk dividing the flower border: yucca, hydrangea, bergenia and stachys.

70

double purpose of keeping the soil cool and of affording gradual nutriment when water is given.

The planting of the border is designed to show a distinct scheme of colour arrangement. At the two ends there is a groundwork of grey and glaucous foliage – *Stachys, Santolina, Senecio cineraria*, sea-kale and Lyme-grass, with darker foliage, also of grey quality, of *Yucca, Clematis recta* and rue. With this, at the near or western end, there are flowers of pure blue, grey-blue, white, palest yellow and palest pink : each colour partly in distinct masses and partly intergrouped. The colouring then passes through stronger yellows to orange and red. By the time the middle space of the border is reached the colour is strong and gorgeous, but, as it is in good harmonies, it is never garish. Then the colour strength recedes in an inverse sequence through orange and deep yellow to pale yellow, white and palest pink ; again with blue-grey foliage. But at this, the eastern end, instead of the pure blues we have purples and lilacs.

Looked at from a little way forward, for a wide space of grass allows this point of view, the whole border can be seen as one picture, the cool colouring at the ends enhancing the brilliant warmth of the middle. Then, passing along the wide path next the border, the value of the colour arrangement is still more strongly felt. Each portion now becomes a picture in itself, and every one is of such a colouring that it best prepares the eye, in accordance with natural law, for what is to follow. Standing for a few moments before the end-most region of grey and blue, and saturating the eye to its utmost capacity with these colours, it passes with extraordinary avidity to the succeeding yellows. These intermingle in a pleasant harmony with the reds and scarlets, blood-reds and clarets, and then lead again to yellows. Now the eye has again become saturated, this time with the rich colouring, and has

Above: Delphinium; below left: *Stachys lanata*; below right: rue.

therefore, by the law of complementary colour, acquired a strong appetite for the greys and purples. These therefore assume an appearance of brilliancy that they would not have had without the preparation provided by their recently received complementary colour.

There are well-known scientific toys illustrating this law. A short word, printed in large red letters, is looked at for half a minute. The eyes are shut and an image of the same word appears, but the lettering is green. Many such experiments may be made in the open garden. The brilliant orange African marigold has leaves of a rather dull green colour. But look steadily at the flowers for thirty seconds in sunshine and then look at the leaves. The leaves appear to be bright blue!

Even when a flower border is devoted to a special season, as mine is given to the time from mid-July to October, it cannot be kept fully furnished without resorting to various contrivances. One of these is the planting of certain things that will follow in season of bloom and that can be trained to take each other's places. Thus, each plant of *Gypsophila paniculata* when full grown covers a space a good four feet

72

wide. On each side of it, within reasonable distance of the root, I plant oriental poppies. These make their leaf and flower growth in early summer when the gypsophila is still in a young state. The poppies will have died down by the time the gypsophila is full grown and has covered them. After this has bloomed the seed-pods turn brown, and though a little of this colouring is not harmful in the autumn border, yet it is not wanted in such large patches. We therefore grow at its foot, or within easy reach, some of the trailing nasturtiums, and lead them up so that they cover the greater part of the brown seed-spray.

Delphiniums, which are indispensable for July, leave bare stems with quickly yellowing leafage when the flowers are over. We plant behind them the white everlasting pea, and again behind that *Clematis* 'Jackmanii'. When the delphiniums are over, the rapidly forming seed-pods are removed, the stems are cut down to just the right height, and the white peas are trained over them. When the peas go out of bloom in the middle of August, the clematis is brought over. It takes some years for these two plants to become established; in the

Left: African marigold; right: *Kniphofia uvaria*.

73

Soft yellow anthemis, thalictrum and santolina, soft pink and white valerian, clary and roses create a misty framework for the spires of the delphiniums. In the foreground stachys completes the picture with its first carpets of felted leaves and woolly spikes of flowers, which echo the vertical lines of the delphiniums and tall grey onopordon.

case of those I am describing the pea has been four or five years planted and the clematis seven. They cannot be hurried; indeed, in my garden it is difficult to get the clematis to grow at all. But good gardening means patience and dogged determination. There must be many failures and losses, but by always pushing on there will also be the reward of success. Those who do not know are apt to think that hardy flower gardening of the best kind is easy. It is not easy at all. It has taken me half a lifetime merely to find out what is best worth doing, and a good slice out of another half to puzzle out the ways of doing it.

In addition to these three plants that I grow over one another I am now adding a fourth – the September-blooming *Clematis flammula*. It must not be supposed that they are just lumped one over another so that the under ones have their leafy growths smothered. They are always being watched, and, bit by bit, the earlier growths are removed as soon as their respective plants are better without them.

Then there is the way of pulling down tall plants whose natural growth is upright. At the back of the yellow part of the border are some plants of a form of *Helianthus salicifolius*, trained down, as described later. But other plants can be treated in the same way; the tall *Rudbeckia* 'Golden Glow', and dahlias and Michaelmas daisies. The tall snapdragons can also be pulled down and made to cover a surprising space of bare ground with flowering side-shoots.

As it is still impossible to prevent the occurrence of a blank here and there, or as the scene, viewed as a picture, may want some special accentuation or colouring, there is the way of keeping a reserve of plants in pots and dropping them in where they may be wanted. The thing that matters is that, in its season, the border shall be kept full and beautiful; by what means does not matter in the least. For this sort of work some of the most useful plants are hydrangeas, *Lilium longiflorum*, *L. candidum* and *L. auratum*, and *Campanula pyramidalis*, both white and blue, and, for foliage, *Hosta plantaginea* var. *grandiflora*, *H. sieboldiana* and hardy ferns.

An important matter is that of staking and supporting. The rule, as I venture to lay it down, is that sticks and stakes must never show. They must be so arranged that they give the needful support, while allowing the plant its natural freedom; but they must remain invisible. The only time when they are tolerated is for the week or two when they have been put in for dahlias, when the plants have not yet

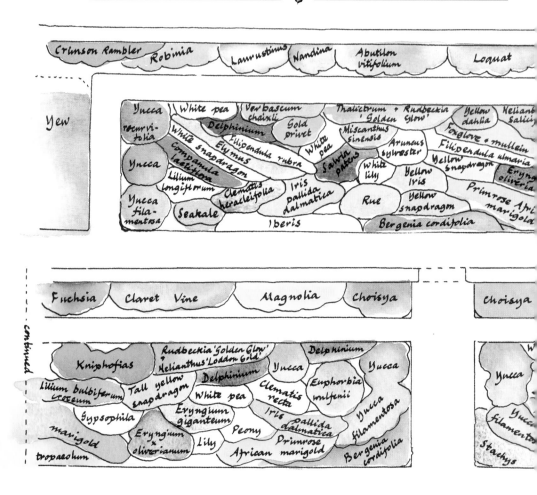

Plan of the main flower
border

grown up to cover them.

Michaelmas daisies we stake with great care in June, putting in some stiff branching spray of oak or chestnut among the growths and under their fronts. At the end of June we also nip the tops of some of the forward growths of the plants so as to vary the outline.

There are two borders of Michaelmas daisies, one for the earlier sorts that flower in September and the other for the October kinds. They are in places that need not often be visited except in the blooming season, therefore we allow the supporting spray to be seen while the plants are growing. But early in August in the case of the September border, and early in September in the case of the one for October, we go round and regulate the plants, settling them among the sticks in their definite

76

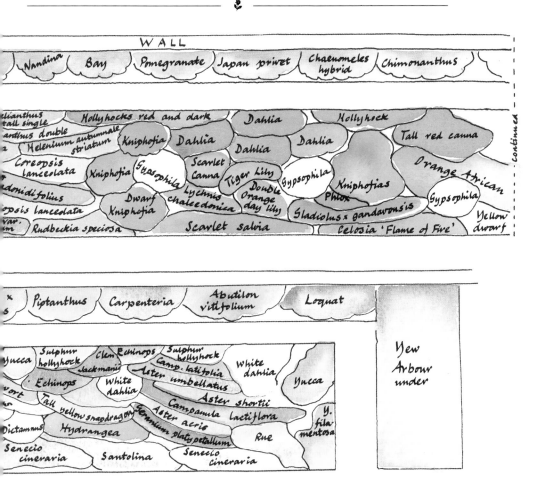

positions. When this is done every atom of projecting spray is cut away with the *secateur*.

I hold that nothing unsightly should be seen in the garden. The shed for sticks and stakes is a lean-to at one end of the barn, showing to the garden. The roof had to be made at a very low pitch, and there was no roofing material suitable but galvanized iron. But a depth of four inches of peaty earth was put over the iron, and now it is a garden of stonecrops and other plants that flourish in shallow soil in a hot exposure.

To prevent undue disappointment, those who wish for beautiful flower borders and whose enthusiasm is greater than their knowledge, should be reminded that if a border is to be planted for pictorial effect,

it is impossible to maintain that effect and to have the space well filled for any period longer than three months, and that even for such a time there will have to be contrivances such as have been described.

It should also be borne in mind that a good hardy flower border cannot be made all at once. Many of the most indispensable perennials take two, three or even more years to come to their strength and beauty. The best way is to plant the border by a definite plan, allowing due space for the development of each plant. Then, for the first year or two, a greater number of half-hardy annuals and biennials than will eventually be needed should be used to fill the spaces that have not yet been taken up by the permanent plants. The best of these are penstemons and snapdragons, the snapdragons grown both as annuals and biennials, for so an extended season of bloom is secured. Then there should be African and French marigolds, the smaller annual sunflowers, zinnias, plume celosias, China asters, stocks, fox-gloves, mulleins, *Ageratum*, *Phlox drummondii* and Indian pinks ; also hardy annuals – lupins of several kinds, *Chrysanthemum coronarium*, the fine pink mallows, love-in-a-mist, nasturtiums or any others that are liked.

Towering delphiniums, *Geranium platypetalum* ('the best of the cranesbills') and peach-leaved campanula furnished the soft blue ends of Miss Jekyll's main flower border with oriental poppies providing brighter accents early in the season.

Chapter VII

THE FLOWER BORDER
IN JULY

OWARDS the end of July the large flower border begins to show its scheme. Until then, although it has been well filled with growing plants, there has been no attempt to show its whole intention. But now this is becoming apparent. The two ends, as already described, are of grey foliage, with, at the near end, flowers of pale blue, white and lightest yellow. The tall spikes of pale blue delphinium are over, and now there are the graceful grey-blue flowers of *Campanula lactiflora* that stand just in front of the great larkspurs. At the back is a white everlasting pea, four years planted and now growing tall and strong. The over-blown flowers of the delphinium have been removed, but their stems have been left just the right height for supporting the growth of the white pea, which is now trained over them and comes forward to meet the pale blue-white campanula. In front of this there is a drift of rue, giving a beautiful effect of dim grey colour and softened shadow; it is crowned by its spreading corymbs of pale yellow bloom that all rise nearly to a level. Again in front is the grand glaucous foliage of sea-kale. A little further along, and towards the back, is a bush of golden privet, taking up and continuing the pale yellow of the rue blossom, and forming a kind of groundwork to a group of the fine mullein *Verbascum phlomoides* now fully out. Just below this is a clump of the double meadowsweet, a mass of warm white flower-foam. Intergrouped are tall snapdragons, white and palest yellow. Then forward are the pale blue-green sword-blades of *Iris pallida* var. *dalmatica* that flowered in June. This is one of the few irises admitted to the border, but it is here because it has the quality, rare among its kind, of maintaining its great leaves in beauty to near the end of the year. Quite to the front are lower-growing plants of purest blue – the Cape daisy (*Felicia amelloides*) and blue lobelia.

Now we pass to a rather large group of *Eryngium × oliverianum*, the

Left to right: *Felicia amelloides, Eryngium × oliverianum* and *Lobelia erinus.*

fine kind that is commonly but wrongly called *E. amethystinum*. It is a deep-rooting perennial that takes three to four years to become strongly established. In front of this are some pale and darker blue spiderworts (*Tradescantia virginiana*), showing best in cloudy weather. At the back is *Thalictrum flavum*, whose bloom is a little overpast, though it still shows some of its foamy-feathery pale yellow. Next we come to stronger yellows, with a middle mass of a good home-grown form of *Coreopsis lanceolata*. This is fronted by a stretch of *Helenium autumnale* var. *pumilum*. Behind the coreopsis are *Achillea filipendulina* and yellow cannas.

Now the colour strengthens with the scarlet balm or bergamot (*Monarda didyma* 'Cambridge Scarlet') intergrouped with *Senecio adonidifolius*, a plant little known but excellent in the flower border. A few belated orange lilies (*Lilium bulbiferum* var. *croceum*) have their colour nearly repeated by the gazanias next to the path. The strong colour is now carried on by *Lychnis chalcedonica*, scarlet salvia, *Lychnis haageana* (a fine plant that is much neglected), and some of the dwarf nasturtiums of brightest scarlet. After this we gradually return to the grey-blues, whites and pale yellows, with another large patch of

81

Eryngium × *oliverianum*, white everlasting pea, *Calceolaria*, and the splendid leaf-mass of a wide and high plant of *Euphorbia wulfenii*, which, with the accompanying yuccas, rises to a height far above my head. Passing between a clump of yuccas on either side is the cross-walk leading by an arched gateway through the wall. The border beyond this is a shorter length, and has a whole ground of grey foliage – *Stachys, Santolina, Elymus, Senecio cineraria*, and sea-kale. Then another group of rue, with grey-blue foliage and pale yellow bloom, shows near the extreme end against the full green of the young summer foliage of the yew arbour that comes at the end of the border. Again at this end is the tall *Campanula lactiflora*. In the nearer middle a large mass of purple clematis is trained over stiff, branching spray, and is beginning to show its splendid colour, while behind, and looking their best in the subdued light of the cloudy morning on which these notes are written, are some plants of *Verbascum phlomoides*, ten feet high, showing a great cloud of pure pale yellow. They owe their vigour to being self-sown seedlings, never transplanted. Instead of having merely a blooming spike, as is the usual way of those that are planted, these have abundant side branches. They dislike bright

Top: *Monarda didyma*; bottom: gazania.

Left to right: Lychnis, salvia and nasturtium.

sunshine, only expanding fully in shade or when the day is cloudy and inclined to be rainy. Close to them, rising to the wall's whole eleven feet of height, is a *Cistus × cyprius*, bearing a quantity of large white bloom with a deep red spot at the base of each petal.

Though there is as yet but little bloom in this end of the border, the picture is complete and satisfying. Each one of the few flower-groups tells to the utmost, while the intervening masses of leafage are in themselves beautiful and have the effect of being relatively well disposed. There is also such rich promise of flower beauty to come that the mind is filled with glad anticipation, besides feeling content for the time being with what it has before it. There is one item of colouring that strikes the trained eye as specially delightful. It is a bushy mass of *Clematis recta*, now out of bloom. It occurs between the overhanging purple clematis and the nearer groups of *Senecio cineraria* and *Santolina*. The leaves are much deeper in tone than these and have a leaden sort of blueness, but the colouring, both of the parts in light and even more of the mysterious shadows, is in the highest degree satisfactory and makes me long for the appreciative presence of those few friends who are artists both on canvas and in their gardens, and most of all for that of one who is now dead [H. B. Brabazon] but to

'Next we come to the stronger yellows'. Helianthus, coreopsis and helenium flow around the spikes of tall yellow loose-strife.

White rose 'La Guirlande': grey borders beyond.

whom I owe, with deepest thankfulness, a precious memory of forty years of helpful and sympathetic guidance and encouragement in the observation and study of colour beauty.

One cannot write of the garden in July without a word on the roses. Besides the bushy garden roses, and the kinds of special charm, such as Damask, Provence, Moss and China, those that most nearly concern the garden for beauty and pictorial effect are the rambling and climbing roses that flower in clusters.

In *Roses for English Gardens* I dealt at some length with the many ways of using them ; here I must only touch upon one or two of these ways. But I wish to remind my readers of the great value of these free roses for running up through such trees as yews or hollies in regions where garden joins hands with woodland, and also of their great usefulness for forming lines of arch and garland as an enclosure to some definite space. I have them like this forming the boundary on two sides of a garden of long beds, whose other two sides are a seven-foot wall and the back of a stable and loft. Just beyond the arch, and dividing the little garden in two, is the short piece of double border that is devoted to August.

Penstemons, geraniums, achilleas, artemisias and other favourites of Miss Jekyll blend in early summer against the creamy white garlands of *Rosa longicuspis*.

The other long beds in this region are for special combinations, some of them of July flowers ; *e.g.*, orange *Lilium bulbiferum* var. *croceum*

84

with the beautiful *Clematis recta*, a plant but little known, though it is easy to grow and is one of the best of summer flowers. One bed is for blue colouring with grey foliage. Here is the lovely Belladonna hybrid delphinium[6], with flowers of a blue purer than that of any other of its beautiful kind. It never grows tall, nor has it the strong, robust aspect of the larger ones, but what it lacks in vigour is more than made up for by the charming refinement of the whole plant. In the same bed are the other pure blues of the rare double Siberian larkspur, and the single allied kind *Delphinium grandiflorum*, of *Salvia patens* and of the Cape daisy (*Felicia amelloides*). Between the clumps of Belladonna are bushes of white lavender, and the whole is carpeted and edged with the white foliage of *Artemisia stelleriana*, the quite hardy plant that is such a good substitute for the tenderer *Senecio cineraria*.

Among the best flowers of July that have a place in this garden are the penstemons planted last year. We grow them afresh from cuttings every autumn, planting them out in April. They are not quite hardy, and a bad winter may destroy all the last year's plants. But if these can be saved they bloom in July, whereas those planted in the spring of the year do not flower till later. So we protect the older plants with fir-

Of the many ways of using roses Miss Jekyll particularly admired 'their great usefulness for forming lines of arch and garland as an enclosure to some definite space'.

Generous groups of grey
foliage with flowers of
blue or purple framed
the main flower border
at Munstead Wood.

boughs and generally succeed in saving them. Old plants of snapdragon are also now in flower. They too are a little tender in the open,
although they are safe in dry-walling with the roots out of the way of
frost and the crowns kept dry among the stones.

Much use is made of a dwarf kind of lavender that is also among the
best of the July flowers. The whole size of the plant is about one-third
that of the ordinary kind ; the flowers are darker in colour and the time
of blooming a good month earlier. It has a different use in gardening,
as the flowers, being more crowded and of a deeper tint, make a distinct colour effect. Besides its border use, it is a plant for dry banks,
tops of rock-work and dry-walling.

Chapter VIII

THE FLOWER BORDER
IN AUGUST

BY the second week of August the large flower border is coming
to its best. The western grey end, with its main planting of
hoary and glaucous foliage – yucca, sea-kale, *Senecio cineraria*,
rue, *Elymus, Santolina, Stachys,* &c. – now has *Yucca flaccida* in flower.
This neat, small yucca, one of the varieties or near relatives of *Y.
filamentosa*, is a grand plant for late summer. A well-established clump
throws up a quantity of flower-spikes of that highly ornamental
character that makes the best of these fine plants so valuable. White
everlasting pea, planted about three feet from the back, is trained on
stout pea-sticks over the space occupied earlier by the delphiniums.
A little of it runs into a bush of golden privet. This golden privet
is one of the few shrubs that have a place in the flower border.
Its clean, cheerful, bright yellow gives a note of just the right colour
all through the summer. It has also a solidity of aspect that enhances
by contrast the graceful lines of the foliage of a clump of the great
Japanese striped grass *Miscanthus sinensis* 'Zebrinus', which stands
within a few feet of it, seven feet high, shooting upright, but with the
ends of the leaves recurved.

Snapdragons, tall white and tall yellow, spire up four feet high, following the earlier foxgloves. At the back is a pretty pink dahlia with
sulphur and pale pink hollyhocks. A little further along, and staked
out so as to take the place of the clumps of *Verbascum chaixii* that were
so fine at the end of June, is an apricot dahlia with a slight pink flush.
Forward is a group of a penstemon of palest pink colouring named
'Evelyn', then a patch or two of palest blue spiderwort[7], and, quite to
the front in any spaces there may be among the grey foliage, *Lobelia*
'Cobalt Blue', the taller *L. tenuior*, and the pretty little blue-flowered
Cape daisy, *Felicia amelloides*.

The whole border is backed by a stone wall eleven feet high, now

fully clothed with shrubs and plants that take their place in the colour
scheme, either for tint of bloom or mass of foliage. Thus the red-leaved
claret vine (*Vitis vinifera* 'Purpurea') shows as background to the rich
red region, and *Robinia hispida* stands where its pink clusters will tell
rightly; *Choisya* and *Cistus* × *cyprius* where their dark foliage and
white bloom will be of value; the greyish foliage and abundant pale
lilac blossom of *Abutilon vitifolium* in the grey and purple region, and
the pale green foliage of the deciduous *Magnolia denudata* showing as a
background to the tender blue of a charming pale delphinium.

The shrubs and plants on the wall are not all there because they are
things rare and precious or absolutely needing the shelter of the wall,
though some of them are glad of it; but because they give a background that either harmonizes in detail with what is in front or will
help to enrich or give general cohesion to the picture. The front of the
border has some important foliage giving a distinctly blue effect,
prominent among it sea-kale. The flower-stems are cut hard back in
the earlier summer, and it is now in handsome fresh leaf. Further back
is the fine blue foliage of lyme-grass (*Elymus arenarius*), a plant of our
sea-shores, but of much value for blue effects in the garden.

Now is the time to begin to use our reserve of plants in pots. Of
these the most useful are the hydrangeas. They are dropped into any
vacant spaces, more or less in groups, in the two ends of the border
where there is grey foliage, their pale pink colouring agreeing with
these places. Their own leafage is a rather bright green, but we get
them so well bloomed that but few leaves are seen, and we arrange as
cleverly as we can that the rest shall be more or less hidden by the
surrounding bluish foliage. I stand a few paces off, directing the
formation of the groups; considering their shape in relation to the
border as a whole. I say to the gardener that I want a hydrangea in such
a place, and tell him to find the nearest place where it can be dropped
in. Sometimes this dropping in, for the pots have to be partly sunk,
comes in the way of some established plant. If it is a deep-rooted
perennial that takes three or four years to come to its strength, like an
eryngium or a dictamnus, of course I avoid encroaching on its root-
room. But if it is a thing that blooms the season after it is planted, and
of which I have plenty in reserve, such as an anthemis, a tradescantia,
or a helenium, I sacrifice a portion of the plant-group, knowing that it
can easily be replaced. But then by August many of the plants have

Pale yellow snapdragon
and pale pink dahlia

89

spread widely above and there is space below. *Lilium longiflorum* in pots is used in the same way, and for the most part in this blue end of the border, though there are also some at the further, purple end, and just a flash of their white beauty in the middle region of strong reds.

In order to use both blue and purple in the flower border, this cool, western, grey-foliaged end has the blues, and the further, eastern end the purples. For although I like to use colour as a general rule in harmonies rather than contrasts, I prefer to avoid, except in occasional details, a mixture of blue and purple. At this end, therefore, there are flowers of pure blue – *Delphinium, Anchusa, Salvia,* blue Cape daisy and *Lobelia,* and it is only when the main mass of blue, of delphiniums and anchusas, is over that even the presence of the pale grey-blue of *Campanula lactiflora* is made welcome. Near the front is another pale grey-blue, that of *Clematis heracleifolia* var. *davidiana,* just showing a few blooms, but not yet fully out.

Now, giving a pleasant rest and refreshment to the eye after the blues and greys, is a well-shaped drift of the pale sulphur African marigold. It was meant to be the dwarf variety, but, as it grows two and a half feet high, it has been pulled down as it grew. Some of it has

Eryngium giganteum and Madonna lilies, an ethereal composition of grey and white much used at Munstead Wood, are warmed in this border by pink lychnis and roses.

Left to right: *Felicia
amelloides, Campanula
lactiflora* and *Salvia
patens*.

been brought down some way over the edge of the path, where it
breaks the general front line pleasantly and shows off its good soft
colouring. We grow only this pale colour and a good form of the
splendid orange. The intermediate one, the full yellow African marigold, has, to my eye, a raw quality that I am glad to avoid, and I have
other plants that give the strong yellow colour better. Now at the back
are some plants of the single Antwerp hollyhock, *Althaea ficifolia*,
white and pale yellow, recalling, as we merge into the stronger
yellows, the colouring of the region just left. They are partly
intergrouped with that excellent plant *Rudbeckia* 'Golden Glow',
brilliant, long-lasting, and capable of varied kinds of useful treatment.

Now we come to a group of the perennial sunflowers; a good form
of the double *Helianthus decapetalus* in front, and behind it the large
single kind of the same plant. By the side of these is a rather large
group of a garden form of *H. salicifolius*. This is one of the perennial
sunflowers that are usually considered not good enough for careful
gardening. It grows very tall, and bears a smallish bunch of yellow
flowers at the top. If this were all it could do, it would not be in my
flower border. But in front of it grows a patch of the fine tansy-like
Achillea filipendulina, and in front of this again a wide-spreading group
of *Eryngium × oliverianum* – beautiful all through July. When the

91

Left to right: canna, hollyhock and dahlia.

bloom of these is done the tall sunflower is trained down over them – this pulling down, as in the case of so many plants, causing it to throw up flower-stalks from the axils of every pair of leaves; so that in September the whole thing is a sheet of bloom. Thus the plant that was hardly worth a place in the border becomes, at its flowering time, one of the brightest ornaments of the garden. Other plants that are in front of the sunflower, that have also passed out of bloom, are the scarlet bee-balm (*Monarda*) and the very useful alpine groundsel (*Senecio adonidifolius*).

Next we have an important group of a large-leaved canna, the handsomest foliage in the border; good to see when the sun is behind and the light comes through the leaves. Here also, at the back, is a patch of hollyhocks – one very dark, almost a claret-red, and a fine, full red inclining to blood-colour. They tower up together and close to them are dahlias[8], the rich red 'Crimson Beauty', deep scarlet 'The Prince', scarlet 'Fire King', and its variety 'Orange Fire King', now the most brilliant piece of colouring in the garden. These lead on to a

A 'mass of bright colouring.' Vivid phlox, dahlias, penstemons, antholyza, golden rod, achillea and crocosmia combine 'in gorgeous company'.

92

gorgeous company – an orange-red phlox, scarlet penstemon, orange African marigold, scarlet gladiolus, and, to the front, a brilliant dwarf scarlet salvia ; *Helenium autumnale* var. *pumilum* and scarlet and orange dwarf nasturtium. Here and there within this mass of bright colouring there is a patch of the fine deep yellow *Coreopsis lanceolata*, a plant of long-enduring bloom, or rather of long succession, for, if the dead flowers are removed, it will look bright for a good three months.

As this gorgeous mass occupies a large space in the flower border, I have thought well to subdue it here and there with the cloudy masses of *Gypsophila paniculata*. Five-year-old plants of this form masses of the pretty mist-like bloom four feet across and as much high. This bold introduction of grey among the colour masses has considerable pictorial value. As the grey changes, towards the end of the month, to a brownish tone, some of the tall nasturtiums are allowed to grow over the bushes of *Gypsophila*.

Left to right: Tall ageratum, pale yellow hollyhock and *Aster acris*.

Now we have got beyond the middle of the length of the border, and the colour changes again to the clear and pale yellows, and then again to the grey foliage as at the beginning. Where this occurs, at a little more than two-thirds of the way along the border, it is crossed by the path, leading, though an archway in the wall closed by a door, to the garden beyond. This cross-path is flanked by groups of yuccas, slightly raised. Yuccas all like a raised mound and some good loam to grow in. I have them here as well as at the two extreme ends of the border. No plants make a handsomer full-stop to any definite garden scheme. The grey treatment comprises the two yucca mounds to right and left of the cross-path; the other grey plants are as before – *Senecio cineraria*, *Santolina*, *Stachys*, *Elymus* and rue – but at this end, besides some plants with white, pink and palest yellow colouring, the other flowers are not blues, but purples, light and dark. Among these a very useful thing is *Ageratum*; not the dwarf ageratum, though this is good too in its place, but the ordinary *Ageratum houstonianum*, a plant that grows about two feet high. This is also the place for some of the earliest Michaelmas daisies that will bloom in September, such as *Aster acris* and *A. frikartii*. At the back there are dahlias, white and pale yellow, with white and sulphur Antwerp hollyhocks, and, in the middle spaces, pale pink gladiolus, double *Saponaria officinalis*, and pale pink penstemon. At the back, also, there is a clump of globe thistle (*Echinops*) and a grand growth of *Clematis* 'Jackmanii', following in season of bloom, and partly led over, a white everlasting pea, that in the earlier summer was trained to conceal the dying stems of the red-orange lilies that bloomed in June.

There is also a short length of double border specially devoted to August, of the same character, though not so fully developed, as what will be described in a further chapter as the Grey Garden. Here, the space being small, it has been given specially to the more restricted season. The scheme of colouring has a ground of grey foliage, with flowers of pink, white, and light and dark purple.

Next the path is the silvery white of *Stachys*, *Senecio cineraria* and *Artemisia stelleriana*, with the grey foliage and faint purple of the second bloom of catmint. Then bushy masses of lavender and *Gypsophila*, and between them *Lilium longiflorum*, *Godetia* 'Double Rose' and white snapdragons. Behind and among these are groups of the clear white *Achillea* 'The Pearl', and the round purple heads of globe

95

thistle. Here and there, pushing to the front, is a silver thistle (*Eryngium giganteum*). At the back shoot up pink hollyhocks, the kind being one of home growth known as 'Pink Beauty'. The deep green of a figtree that covers the upper part of the landing and outside stone steps to a loft, is an excellent background to the tender greys of these August borders. Unfortunately, the main group of pink hollyhock that should have stood up straight and tall and shown well against the window and silvery-grey weather-boarding of the loft, failed altogether last season; in fact, all the hollyhocks were poor and stunted, so that an important part of the intended effect was lost.

Of late years there have been some useful additions to this special August border, the most notable being the bushy pink-flowered *Lavatera olbia*, all the more valuable because there are not many flowers of pink colouring for the time of year. Another useful acquisition among the cool pinks is one of Messrs Cheal's star dahlias, named 'Ifield Star'. Towards the back, among the echinops we also use the white star dahlias, taking care to plant them within hand reach, because, in common with all their kind, their bloom is so much increased and prolonged by keeping the exhausted flowers cut out. Also towards the back there are some bushes of *Ceanothus* 'Gloire de

The Grey borders: stachys, gypsophila, lily, *Achillea* 'The Pearl' and pink hollyhocks.

Ceanothus 'Gloire de Versailles' and silver buckthorn (*Hippophaë rhamnoides*).

Versailles', whose grey-blue flowers are just right, and *Clematis* 'Jackmanii', which is trained into supporting clumps of the grey-leaved sea buckthorn. In this garden the *Clematis* 'Jackmanii' is in all cases the plant in the original fine purple colouring, not the so-called improved of a deeper and more reddish tint. Here we want the clearer purple of cooler tone.

Of lavender hedges there are several, of varying ages, in different parts of the garden. Lavender for cutting should be from plants not more than four to five years old, but for pictorial effect the bushes may be much older. When they are growing old it is a good plan to plant white and purple clematis so that they can be trained freely through and over them.

There are comparatively few shrubs that flower in autumn, so that it is quite a pleasant surprise to come upon a group of them all in bloom together. The picture shows the satisfactory effect of a group of *Æsculus parviflora* and *Olearia haastii*. It would have been all the better for some plants of the beautiful blue-flowered *Perovskia atriplicifolia* and for *Caryopteris × clandonensis* in front, but at the time of planting I did not think of the caryopteris and did not know the perovskia.

August is the month of China asters. I find many people are shy of these capital plants, perhaps because the mixtures, such as are commonly grown, contain rather harsh and discordant colours ; also perhaps because a good many of the kinds, having been purposely dwarfed in order to fit them for pot-culture and bedding, are too stiff to look pretty in general gardening. Such kinds will always have their uses, but what is wanted now in the best gardening is more freedom of habit. I have a little space that I give entirely to China asters. I have often had the pleasure of showing it to some person who professed a dislike to them, and with great satisfaction have heard them say, with true admiration : 'Oh ! but I had no idea that China asters could be so beautiful.'

Roses, alchemilla and lavender in the summer garden. 'Of lavender hedges there are several, of varying ages, in different parts of the garden'.

Caryopteris × *clandonensis*, tree mallow (*Lavatera olbia*) and *Perovskia atriplicifolia*.

Chapter IX

BEDDING PLANTS

THIS is a conveniently comprehensive term for the tender plants that are put out for the summer. To these plants a small portion of my garden, well sheltered within enclosing walls and yet open to full sunshine, is devoted, so that the little place is in some kind of beauty from the end of July to the last days of September. There has been so strong a revulsion in garden practice since the days when the bedding out of tender plants in stiff and not very intelligent ways absorbed the entire horticultural energy of owners of gardens that many people have conceived a dislike to the plants themselves. It is a common thing for friends to express surprise at seeing scarlet geraniums, yellow *Calceolaria* and blue *Lobelia* in my garden, forgetting that it was not the fault of the plants that they were misused or employed in dull or even stupid ways. There are no better summer flowers than the single and double zonal pelargoniums that we commonly call geraniums, and none so good for such uses as the filling of tubs and vases; for not only do they enjoy full sunlight, but they benefit by the extra warmth at the root that they obtain by being raised in the warm air above the ground level. There certainly are among these good summer flowers, a few kinds of harsh, unpleasant reds and pinks, but these are easily avoided, and the range of good colouring, from purest scarlet, through softer tones, to tints of salmon and tender warm pink, is now so great that there is no difficulty in obtaining any combination or sequence that may be desired, such as the very simple one that is shown in the plan and will presently be described.

The little garden is an odd-shaped piece of ground, roughly triangular. The main clump is more than thirty feet wide at one end, a width too great to treat conveniently. It has therefore been arranged with a kind of elevated backbone, a few feet wide, raised less than two feet above the level, with dry walling on each side to retain the earth. As it approaches the narrow end of the triangle it swings round symmetrically on each side forward to the path. All this raised part is treated quite differently to the rest of the garden. There is no attempt at brilliant colouring, but rather to have important masses of fine form in a quiet range of greyish tinting that shall serve as a suitable background to the brighter effects. The planting is mainly of yuccas of both large and small kinds and of two kinds of euphorbia; the bold and striking *E. wulfenii* with its handsome form of leaf-mass and

Zonal pelargoniums of graded colours.

immense bloom, and the smaller *E. characias.* Where the walls come near the path there are hanging sheets of the bluish grey foliage of *Othonnopsis cheirifolia.* The raised mass is fairly wide at the south-western end. Spaces next the path are filled with flowers of pink and purple colouring such as heliotrope, ivy geranium 'Mme Crousse' and *Verbena* 'Miss Willmott'. The star-shaped figures on the plan show the yuccas: the larger ones are *Y. gloriosa* and *Y. recurvifolia*, and the smaller, garden varieties of *Y. filamentosa.* There is always a good proportion of yuccas in bloom during the late summer, so that, standing at the north-west corner, the stately flower spikes have a fine effect rising above the colour masses of the borders on the lower level.

These are in two main connected colour schemes – in gradations of reds, and of whites and yellows respectively. In the red portions the front is chiefly of geraniums; 'Paul Crampel' for the strongest red; it is a little softer and more pleasing to me than 'Raspail', which we formerly used. My eye has had too much tender tutoring to endure the

Penstemons, a most
useful plant for filling
gaps in the border, here
combine with lavender
and *Spiraea bumalda* in a
setting of grey foliage.

popular 'Henry Jacoby' – a colour that, for all its violence, has a harsh
dullness that I find displeasing. Next to 'Paul Crampel' we put one of
the softer reds such as 'Dot Slade', and this leads to the fine salmon-
coloured 'King of Denmark', and then to the paler salmon pink of
'Salmon Fringed', a plant that has the additional advantage of a
beautifully zoned leaf. Some such arrangement is followed throughout
those portions of the garden where red colouring prevails; the plants
for the back being three varieties of red-bloomed cannas, one of them
with well-coloured red foliage, and a larger growing kind with great
leaves so much like those of a banana that, having lost its original
name, we know it as 'Canna Musa'. This has the leaves slightly red-
tinted. With these cannas, arranged as shown in the plan, are thin
drifts of *Gladiolus* × *gandavensis* and others of near colouring, among
them the very fine and free *G*. × *childsii* 'William Faulkner'; also the
best of the scarlet and orange-scarlet dahlias, both of the larger-
flowered and pompon kinds, scarlet penstemon, *Alonsoa*, *Lobelia
cardinalis*, and, behind the geraniums, *Salvia* 'Pride of Zurich'. In
several places among the reds comes a drift of a fine garden form of the
native *Sedum telephium*. The quiet grey-green of the plant turns to a
subdued chocolate-red, as the large, flat flower-head is developed. The
introduction of this undergrowth of quieter related colouring greatly
enhances the quality of the livelier reds and helps to put the whole
thing together. One break of a white lily (*L. longiflorum*) comes with
fine effect among the reds.

Another plant that we find of much use as an undergrowth among
the flowers is a dwarf form of the old love-lies-bleeding (*Amaranthus*)
that I have only been able to obtain from Messrs Vilmorin of Paris,
their *Amaranthus sanguineus* var. *nanus*[9]. Its height is not much over a
foot; the foliage inclines to a reddish tint and the flower, instead of
being magenta, as in our more familiar plant, is of a quiet dusky red,
that forms an admirably harmonious setting to flowers of warm rich
colouring. It has the effect of a warm underglow that is singularly
pleasing and effective. It is necessary to sow it in place.

The yellow and white portions pass from the palest of the geraniums
with a front planting of the useful, but in the past much misused,
golden-feather feverfew, and a rather large quantity of a capital old
garden plant, that has of late been much neglected, the variegated
form of a native plant *Mentha rotundifolia*. The feverfew is allowed to

Top to bottom: Golden feverfew, *Lilium longiflorum* and variegated apple-mint (*Mentha rotundifolia* 'Variegata').

The garden of summer flowers

flower, but the variegated mint has the flowering branches cut back so as to keep it to a more convenient height. It is one of the prettiest things as an underplanting to anything of white or yellow colour, and specially charming among the white lilies (*L. longiflorum*); here and there it is brightened with thin drifts of the pale canary-yellow *Calceolaria amplexicaulis*. The plan shows the general arrangement of the other white and yellow flowers; yellow-bloomed cannas both tall and short, snapdragons white, lemon-white and yellow, and primrose African marigold. It needs some care to obtain the right colour of this marigold. There are three distinct colourings of this fine half-hardy annual – the well-known deep orange, a middle yellow and the primrose. Unless the primrose or sulphur colour is insisted on seedsmen are apt to send the middle colour. I have it always from Messrs Barr and Sons, who send the right colour without fail.

104

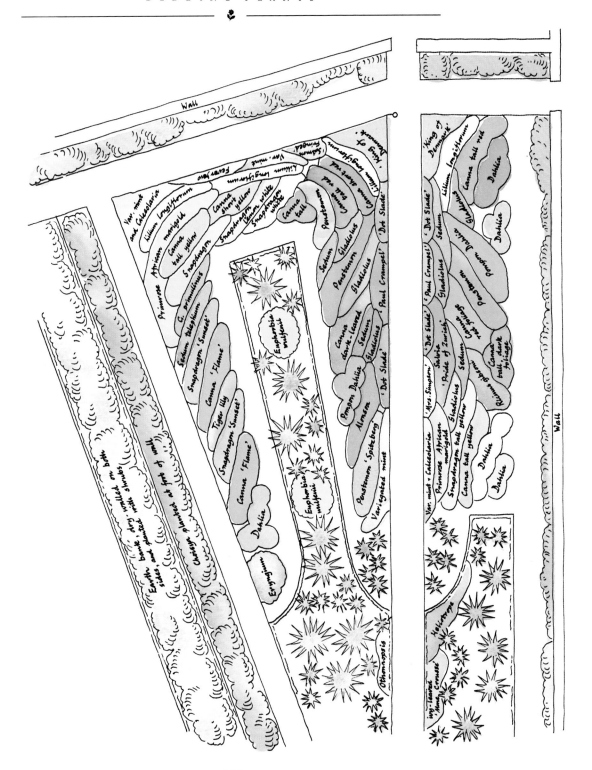

Chapter X

THE FLOWER BORDERS
IN SEPTEMBER

THE main flower border shows in September much the same aspect as in August. But early in the month the middle mass of strong colouring, enhanced by kniphofias and the fuller bloom of dahlias, is at its brightest. The bold masses of canna foliage have also grown up and show their intended effect. They form one of the highest points in the border. No attempt is made to keep all the back-row plants standing high; on the contrary, many that would be the tallest are pulled down to do colour work of medium height. The effect is much more pictorial when the plants at the back rise only here and there to a height of nine or ten feet; mounting gradually and by no means at equal distances, but somewhat as the forms of greater altitude rise in the ridge of a mountain range.

Rather near the front, the bushy masses of *Gypsophila*, which a month ago were silvery grey, have now turned to a brownish colour. They are partly covered with trailing nasturtiums, but the portions of brown cloud that remain tone well with the rich reds that are near them. In the back of this region dark claret and blood-red hollyhocks still show colour, and scarlet dahlias are a mass of gorgeous bloom. Their nearest neighbours are tall flaming kniphofias, with, in front of them, one of the dwarfer kniphofias that is crowded with its orange-scarlet flowers of a rather softer tone. Then come scarlet gladiolus, a wide group of a splendid red penstemon, and, to the front, an edging and partly carpeting mass of the good, short-growing form of *Salvia splendens* called 'Pride of Zurich'.

After these strong reds comes a drift of the brilliant orange African marigold, one of the most telling plants of the time of year. Coming to the yellows of middle strength, there are some of the perennial sunflowers, among them the one that seems to be a form of *Helianthus salicifolius*, described in the last chapter. This and some others are

Pale-pink gladiolus and *Clematis heracleifolia* 'Davidiana'.

106

trained down to cover plants now out of bloom. The fine double rudbeckia called 'Golden Glow' is treated in the same way. Inter-grouped with it is a useful pale form of *Helianthus laetiflorus*, *H.l.* 'Loddon Gold', that takes up the colour when the rudbeckia is failing. In the near end region of blue-grey foliage the bloom of *Clematis heracleifolia* var. *davidiana*, also of a greyish blue, but of a colour quality that is almost exclusively its own, tones delightfully with its nearest neighbours of leaf and bloom. About here some pots of *Plumbago capense* are dropped in; their wide-ranging branches, instead of being stiffly tied, are trained over some bushy plants of leaden-blue-foliaged rue. Near this, and partly shooting up through some of the same setting, are the spikes of a beautiful gladiolus of pale, cool pink colour, the much-prized gift of an American garden-loving friend. Tall white snapdragons, five feet high, show finely among the grace-fully recurved leaves of the blue lyme-grass. Beyond is a group of *Lilium auratum*, and in the more distant front, pale sulphur African marigold, just now at its best.

The further end of the border also has grey foliage associated with pink hydrangeas, white and pink snapdragons, white dahlias, purple

clematis, *Lilium auratum* and *Aster acris*. *Yucca flaccida* is still in beauty.

There is another range of double border for the month of September alone. It passes down through the middle of the kitchen garden and is approached by an arch of laburnum. It is backed on each side by a hornbeam hedge some five and a half feet high. This border is mainly for the earlier Michaelmas daisies ; those that bloom in the first three weeks of the month. Grey foliage in plenty is to the front. Running in between the groups is *Artemisia stelleriana*, the quite hardy plant that so well imitates *Senecio cineraria* ; there are also *Stachys* and white pink. Further back among the flowers are drifts of the grey-blue lyme-grass, some grey bushes of *Phlomis* and a silvery-leaved willow, kept to a suitable size by careful pruning.

The scheme of colouring consists of this groundwork of grey foliage, with white, lilac, purple and pale pink flower ; and, breaking into this colouring in two or three distinct places, flowers of pale yellow and yellowish white with suitable accompanying leafage. There is also, in quite another part of the garden, a later border of other Michaelmas daisies that will follow this in time of blooming. But the September borders have a very different appearance because of their flowers of

Left: *Sedum spectabile*;
right: Japanese
anemone.

108

Left to right: *Clematis* 'Jackmanii', white antirrhinum and pink hydrangea.

pink and yellow, colours which are absent in those of the later season.

The yellow flowers are the pale sulphur African marigold and pale yellow and whitish-yellow tall snapdragons, with bordering masses of variegated coltsfoot, and the golden-feather feverfew allowed to bloom. The pink colourings are the wide-headed *Sedum spectabile*, pink Japanese anemone and a few pale pink gladioli. The whites are dahlias, *Chrysanthemum uliginosum*, the charming perennial aster 'Colerette Blanche' and a taller white or yellowish-white aster with rough stems and harsh-feeling foliage that I know as *A. umbellatus*[10]. Here also are white Japanese anemones, white snapdragons and white China asters. Among the grey bordering plants are groups of dwarf ageratum, one of the best of the tender plants of September and quite excellent with the accompanying grey foliage. The grey bordering is not merely an edging but a general front groundwork, running here and there a yard deep into the border.

Begonias are at their best throughout the month of September. Beds of begonias alone never seem to me quite satisfactory. Here there

(Far left) Borders of Michaelmas daisies with other flowers of soft blue and pink colouring.

Begonias in a setting of bergenia foliage.

is no opportunity for growing them in beds, but I have them in a bit of narrow border that is backed by shrubs that is kept constantly enriched. A groundwork of the large-leaved form of *Bergenia cordifolia* is planted so as to surround variously sized groups of begonias – groups of from five to nine plants. The setting of the more solid leaves gives the begonias a better appearance and makes their bright bloom tell more vividly. They follow in this sequence of colouring: yellow, white, palest pink, full pink, rose, deep red, deep rose, salmon-rose, red-lead colour or orange-scarlet, scarlet, red-lead and orange.

Chapter XI

WOOD AND SHRUBBERY EDGES

OPPORTUNITIES for good gardening are so often overlooked that it may be well to draw attention to some of those that are most commonly neglected.

When woodland joins garden ground there is too often a sudden jolt; the wood ends with a hard line, sometimes with a path along it, accentuating the defect. When the wood is of Scots pine of some age there is a monotonous emptiness of naked trunk and bare ground. In wild moorland this is characteristic and has its own beauty; it may even pleasantly accompany the garden when there is only a view into it here and there; but when the path passes along, furlong after furlong, with no attempt to bring the wood into harmony with the garden, then the monotony becomes oppressive and the sudden jolt is unpleasantly perceived. There is the well-stocked garden and there is the hollow wood with no cohesion between the two – no sort of effort to make them join hands.

It would have been better if from the first the garden had not been brought quite so close to the wood, then the space between, anything from twenty-five to forty feet, might have been planted so as to bring them into unison. In such a case the path would go, not next the trees, but along the middle of the neutral ground, and would be so planted as to belong equally to garden and wood. The trees would then take their place as the bounding and sheltering feature. It is better to plan it like this at first than to gain the space by felling the outer trees, because the trees at the natural wood edge are better furnished with side branches. Such ground on the shady side of the Scots pines would be the best possible site for a rhododendron walk, and for azaleas and kalmias, kept distinct from the rhododendrons. Then the Scots pine indicates the presence of a light peaty soil; the very thing for that excellent but much-neglected undershrub *Gaultheria shallon*. This is one

For the woodland edge Miss Jekyll admired especially the hardy ferns and 'foliage of rather distinct and important size or form'. *Gunnera*, seen here among hardy ferns, would not grow on her dry sand but is ideal for the woodland edge on wetter soils.

113

To reduce the solidity of rhododendrons, Miss Jekyll recommended that they be widely spaced and interplanted with ferns, lilies and other graceful plants. Here, primulas, iris and hostas add to the delicacy of the woodland scene.

of the few things that will grow actually under the Pines, not perhaps in the densest part of an old wood, but anywhere about its edges, or where any light comes in at a clearing or along a cart-way. When once established it spreads with a steady abundance of increase, creeping underground and gradually clothing more and more of the floor of the wood.

The great wood-rush (*Luzula maxima*) is also a capital plant for filling bare spaces in wood edges. It does not look like a rush, but like a broad-leaved grass. The flowers come in May ; loose, spreading clusters of brownish bloom that rise a good two feet above the tufts of handsome foliage.

Rhododendrons are usually planted much too close together. This is a great mistake ; they should not be nearer than eight to ten feet, or even further, apart, especially in the case of *R. ponticum* and some of the larger-growing kinds. It is a common practice to fill up the edges of their prepared places with a collection of heaths. The soil will no doubt suit heaths, but I never do it or recommend it because I feel that the right place for heaths is quite open ground, and there are other plants that I think look better with the young rhododendrons. For my own liking the best of these are hardy ferns – male fern, lady fern and dilated shield fern, with groups of lilies ; *Lilium longiflorum* and the lovely rosy *L. rubellum* towards the front, and *L. auratum* further back. Some species of *Leucothoë*, especially *L. fontanesiana* and *L. axillaris*, are capital plants for this use. Besides lilies, a few other flowering plants suitable for the rhododendron walk are : white foxgloves, white columbine, white *Epilobium angustifolium, Trillium, Epimedium pinnatum, Uvularia grandiflora, Dentaria diphylla* and *Gentiana asclepiadea*. In the same region, and also partly as edgings to the rhododendron clumps, suitable small bushes are *Rhododendron* 'Myrtifolium', the alpenrose (*R. ferrugineum*) and the sweet-leaved *Ledum palustre*.

Later it was found that these wood-path edges offered such suitable places for the late-blooming willow gentian (*Gentiana asclepiadea*), that it was still more largely planted. It delights in a cool place in shade or half-shade, and when in mid-September so many flowers are over and garden plants in general are showing fatigue and exhaustion, it is a pleasure to come upon the graceful arching sprays, their upper portions set with pairs of long blue flowers, looking fresh and bright and full of vigour.

Top to bottom: Male
fern (*Dryopteris filix-mas*),
Lilium auratum and
willow gentian
(*Gentiana asclepiadea*).

When the garden comes on the sunny side of the wood the planting would be quite different. Here is the place for cistuses; for the bolder groups the best are *C. laurifolius* and *C. × cyprius*, backed by plantings of tamarisk, *Arbutus* and white broom, with here and there a free-growing rose of the wilder sort, such as the type *R. multiflora* and *R. brunonii*. If the pine-boughs come down within reach, the wild clematis (*C. vitalba*) can be led into them; it will soon ramble up the tree, filling it with its pretty foliage and abundance of August bloom.

The cistuses delight in a groundwork of heath; the wild calluna looks as well as any, but if cultivated kinds are used they should be in good quantities of one sort at a time, and never as hard edgings, but as free carpeting masses.

116

For the edges of other kinds of woodland the free roses are always beautiful ; where a holly comes to the front, a rose such as 'Sanders' White Rambler' or 'The Garland' will grow up it, supported by its outer branches in the most delightful way. The wild clematis is in place here too, also the shade-loving plants already named. In deciduous woodland there is probably some undergrowth of hazel, or of bramble and wild honeysuckle. White foxgloves should be planted at the edge and a little way back, daffodils for the time when the leaves are not yet there, and lily of the valley, whose charming bloom and brilliant foliage come with the young leaves of May.

Where the wood comes nearest the house with only lawn between, it is well to have a grouping of hardy ferns and lilies ; where it is giving

Left: *Gaultheria shallon*; right: *Bergenia cordifolia*

place to garden ground and there is a shrubby background, the smaller polygonums, such as *P. cuspidatum* var. *compactum*, are in place.

The spaces more or less wide between large shrubs and turf are full of opportunities for ingenious treatment ; they are just the places most often neglected, or at any rate not well enough considered. I have always taken delight in working out satisfactory ways of treating them. It seems desirable to have, next the grass, some foliage of rather distinct and important size or form. For this use the bergenias are invaluable, the one most generally useful being the large variety of *B. cordifolia*. Hostas are also beautiful, but as their leaves come late and go with the first frosts or even earlier, whereas the bergenias persist the whole year round, the latter are the most generally desirable. These shrub-edge spaces occur for the most part in bays, giving an inducement to invent a separate treatment for each bay.

For example, there is a front planting of *Hosta sieboldiana* in two ad-

Gypsophila and bergenia
at the shrubbery edge.

joining bays; in the first, the charming shrubby *Olearia* 'Scilloniensis' flowers in the middle of June; in the other, some groups of *Lilium longiflorum*, planted in November of the year before, are in bloom in early August.

Sometimes a single plant of *Gypsophila paniculata* will fill the whole of one of the recesses or bays between the larger shrubs; *Hydrangea paniculata* is another good filling plant, and the hardy fuchsias; both of these, though really woody shrubs, being cut down every winter and treated as herbaceous plants.

There is a small-growing perennial aster, *A. divaricatus*, from a foot to eighteen inches high, that seems to enjoy close association with other plants and is easy to grow anywhere. I find it, in conjunction with bergenia, one of the most useful of these filling plants for edge spaces that just want some pretty trimming but are not wide enough for anything larger. The same group was photographed two years running. The first year the bloom was a little thicker below, but the second I thought it still better when it had partly rambled up into the lower branches of the weigela that stood behind it. The little thin starry flower is white and is borne in branching heads; the leaves are

118

Miss Jekyll had favourite plants for reducing the massiveness of rhododendrons: 'for my own liking the best of these are hardy ferns' — seen here with the feathery heads of fern-like *Thalictrum aquilegifolium*.

lance-shaped and sharply pointed ; but when the plant is examined in the hand its most distinct character is the small fine wire-like stem, smooth and nearly black, that branches about in an angular way of its own.

These are only a very few examples of what may also be done in a number of other ways, but if they serve to draw attention to those generally neglected shrub edges, it may be to the benefit of many gardens. Where there is room for a good group of plants they should be of bold and solid habit, such as tree lupin, peony, *Acanthus, Aruncus sylvester*, the larger hardy ferns, *Rubus parvifolius*, or plants of some such size and character. The low-growing *Sasa tessellata* is a capital shrub-edge plant.

Chapter XII

GARDENS OF SPECIAL
COLOURING

IT is extremely interesting to work out gardens in which some
special colouring predominates, and to those who, by natural en-
dowment or careful eye-cultivation, possess or have acquired
what artists understand by an eye for colour, it opens out a whole new
range of garden delights.

Arrangements of this kind are sometimes attempted, for occasionally I hear of a garden for blue plants, or a white garden, but
I think such ideas are but rarely worked out with the best aims. I have
in mind a whole series of gardens of restricted colouring, though
I have not, alas, either room or means enough to work them out for
myself, and have to be satisfied with an all-too-short length of double
border for a grey scheme. But besides my small grey garden I badly
want others, and especially a gold garden, a blue garden and a green
garden; though the number of these desires might easily be
multiplied.

It is a curious thing that people will sometimes spoil some garden
project for the sake of a word. For instance, a blue garden, for beauty's
sake, may be hungering for a group of white lilies, or for something of
palest lemon-yellow, but it is not allowed to have it because it is called
the blue garden, and there must be no flowers in it but blue flowers.
I can see no sense in this; it seems to me like fetters foolishly self-
imposed. Surely the business of the blue garden is to be beautiful as
well as to be blue. My own idea is that it should be beautiful first, and
then just as blue as may be consistent with its best possible beauty.
Moreover, any experienced colourist knows that the blues will be more
telling – more purely blue – by the juxtaposition of rightly placed
complementary colour. How it may be done is shown in the plan, for,
as I cannot have these gardens myself, it will be some consolation to
suggest to those who may be in sympathy with my views, how they

Left to right: Golden
holly, spartium and
helianthus.

may be made.

The Grey garden is so called because most of its plants have grey foliage, and all the carpeting and bordering plants are grey or whitish. The flowers are white, lilac, purple and pink. It is a garden mostly for August, because August is the time when the greater number of suitable plants are in bloom ; but a Grey garden could also be made for September, or even October, because of the number of Michaelmas daisies that can be brought into use.

A plan is given of a connected series of gardens of special colouring. For the sake of clearness they are shown in as simple a form as possible, but the same colour scheme could be adapted to others of more important design and larger extent.

The Gold garden is chosen for the middle, partly because it contains the greater number of permanent shrubs and is bright and cheerful all the year round, and partly because it is the best preparation, according to natural colour law, for the enjoyment of the compartments on either side. It is supposed that the house is a little way away to the north, with such a garden scheme close to it as may best suit its style and calibre. Then I would have a plantation of shrubs and trees. The shade and solidity of this would rest and refresh the eye and mind, making

The Orange garden

them the more ready to enjoy the colour garden. Suddenly entering the Gold garden, even on the dullest day, will be like coming into sunshine. Through the shrub-wood there is also a path to right and left parallel to the long axis of the colour garden, with paths turning south at its two ends, joining the ends of the colour-garden paths. This has been taken into account in arranging the sequence of the compartments.

The hedges that back the borders and form the partitions are for the most part of yew, grown and clipped to a height of seven feet. But in the case of the Gold garden, where the form is larger and more free than in the others, there is no definite hedge, but a planting of un-

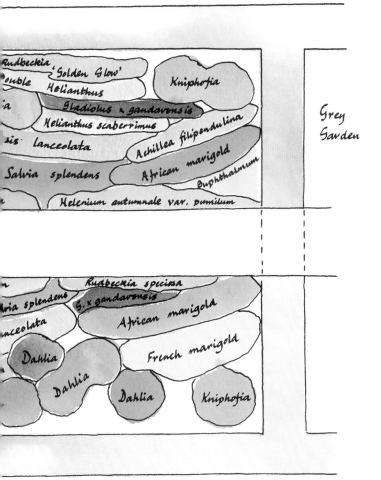

Grey
Garden

Rudbeckia,
'Golden Glow'
ouble Helianthus
Kniphofia
-a
Gladiolus × gandavensis
Helianthus scaberrimus
-sis lanceolata
Achillea filipendulina
Salvia splendens
African marigold
Buphthalmum
Helenium autumnale var. pumilum

Rudbeckia speciosa
-via splendens
G. × gandavensis
-anceolata
African marigold
Dahlia
French marigold
Dahlia
Dahlia
Kniphofia

clipped larger gold hollies, and the beautiful golden plane, so cut back and regulated as to keep within the desired bounds. This absence of a stiff hedge gives more freedom of aspect and a better cohesion with the shrub-wood.

In the case of the Grey garden the hedge is of tamarisk (*Tamarix gallica*), whose feathery grey-green is in delightful harmony with the other foliage greys. It will be seen on the plan that where this joins the Gold garden the hedge is double, for it must be of gold holly on one side and of tamarisk on the other. At the entrances and partition where the path passes, the hedge shrubs are allowed to grow higher, and are eventually trained to form arches over the path.

Special colour garden –
general plan

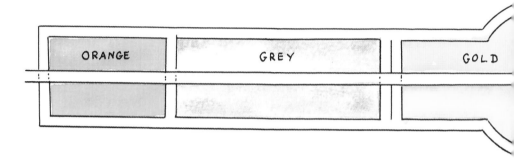

ORANGE · GREY · GOLD

A quarter of the Gold
garden

Tamarisk · Gold holly · Gold holly · Holly · Holly · Ho · Spanish broom · Elaeagnus · Gold elder · Hollyhock · Gold p · Snapdragon · Cassinia fulvida · Cann · African marigold · Small

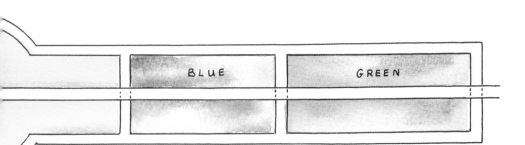

BLUE

GREEN

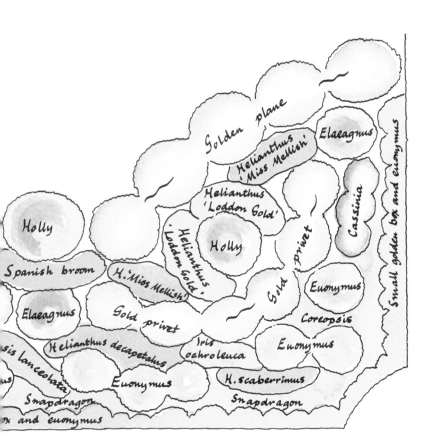

Golden plane

Elaeagnus

Helianthus 'Miss Mellish'

Helianthus 'Loddon Gold'

Cassinia

Holly

Gold Privet

Holly

Helianthus 'Loddon Gold'

Spanish broom

H.'Miss Mellish'

Euonymus

Elaeagnus

Gold privet

Coreopsis

...sis lanceolata

Helianthus decapetalus

Iris ochroleuca

Euonymus

Snapdragon

Euonymus

H. scaberrimus

...x and euonymus

Snapdragon

Small golden box and euonymus

125

'Suddenly entering the Gold garden, even on the dullest day, will be like coming into sunshine'. 'Gold King' holly provides its sunshine the whole year round, and yellow potentillas do so for much of the summer and autumn.

In the Gold and Green gardens the shrubs, which form the chief part of the planting, are shown as they will be after some years' growth. It is best to have them so from the first. If, in order to fill the space at once, several are planted where one only should eventually stand, the extra ones being removed later, the one left probably does not stand quite right. I strongly counsel the placing of them singly at first, and that until they have grown, the space should be filled with temporary plants. Of these, in the Gold garden, the most useful will be *Œnothera erythrosepala, Verbascum olympicum* and *V. phlomoides*, with more Spanish broom than the plan shows till the gold hollies are grown ; and yellow-flowered annuals, such as the several kinds of *Chrysanthemum coronarium*, both single and double, and *Coreopsis drummondii* ; also a larger quantity of African marigolds, the pale primrose and the lemon-coloured. The fine tall yellow snapdragons will also be invaluable. Flowers of a deep orange colour, such as the orange African marigold, so excellent for their own use, are here out of place, only those of pale and middle yellow being suitable.

In such a garden it will be best to have, next the path, either a whole edging of dwarf, gold-variegated box-bushes about eighteen inches to two feet high, or a mixed planting of these and small bushes

October border of Michaelmas daisies.

126

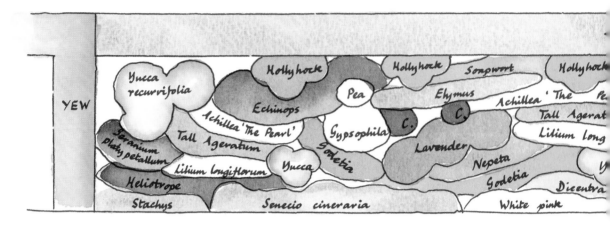

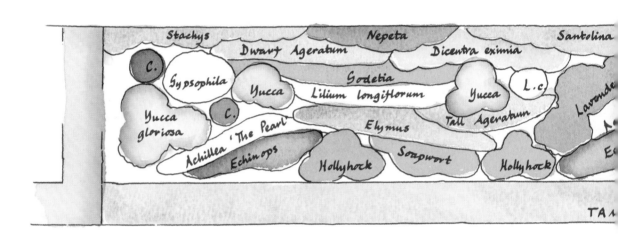

of gold-variegated *Euonymus* clipped down to not much over two feet. The edge next the path would be kept trimmed to a line.

The strength of colour and degree of variation are so great that it is well worth going to a nursery to pick out all these gold-variegated plants. It is not enough to tell the gardener to get them. There should be fervour on the part of the garden's owner such as will take him on a gold-plant pilgrimage to all good nurseries within reach, or even to some rather out of reach. No good gardening comes of not taking pains. All good gardening is the reward of well-directed and strongly sustained effort.

Where, in the Gold garden, the paths meet and swing round in a

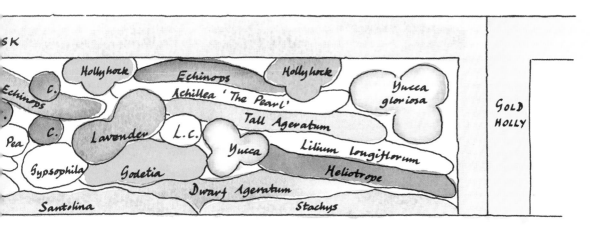

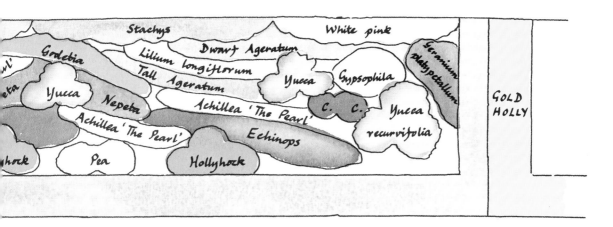

The Grey garden

circle, there may be some accentuating ornament – a sundial, a stone vase for flowers, or a tank for a yellow water-lily. If a sundial, and there should be some incised lettering, do not have the letters gilt because it is the Gold garden ; the colour and texture of gilding are quite out of place. If there is a tank, do not have goldfish ; their colour is quite wrong. Never hurt the garden for the sake of the tempting word.

The word 'gold' in itself is, of course, an absurdity ; no growing leaf or flower has the least resemblance to the colour of gold. But the word may be used because it has passed into the language with a commonly accepted meaning.

129

The Blue garden

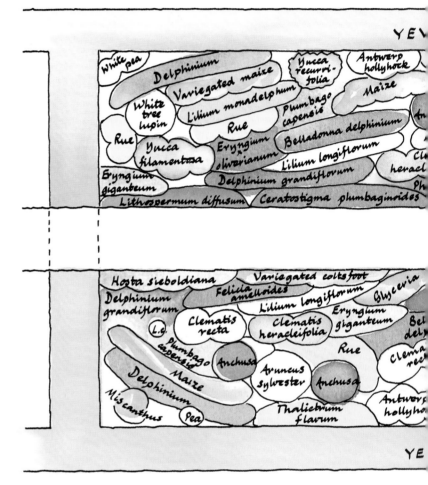

I have always felt a certain hesitation in using the free-growing perennial sunflowers. For one thing, the kinds with the running roots are difficult to keep in check, and their yearly transplantation among other established perennials is likely to cause disturbance and injury to their neighbours. Then, in so many neglected gardens they have been let run wild, surviving when other plants have been choked, that, half unconsciously, one has come to hold them cheap and unworthy of the best use. I take it that my own impression is not mine alone, for often when I have been desired to do planting-plans for flower borders, I have been asked not to put in any of these sunflowers, because 'they are so common.'

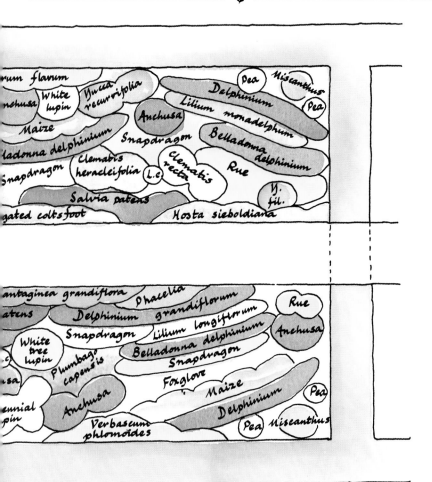

But nothing is 'common' in the sense of base or unworthy if it is rightly used, and it seems to me that this Gold garden is just the place where these bright autumn flowers may be employed to great advantage. I have therefore shown *Helianthus scaberrimus* and its tall-growing variety 'Miss Mellish'[11], although the colour of both is quite the deepest I should care to advise; the paler yellow of *H. laetiflorus* being better, especially 'Loddon Gold', the capital pale form of this sunflower, and of one that I know as a variety of *H. salicifolius*.

The golden planes, where the path comes in from the north, are of course deciduous, and it might be well to have gold hollies again at the back of these, or gold yews, to help the winter effect.

A quantity of grey foliage with blue flowers: artemisia, achillea, nepeta and valerian provide the ideal setting for blue delphiniums and veronica. The sharp yellow flowers of hemerocallis in the background recall the yellow flowers of grey-leaved rue in the border at Munstead Wood.

In some places in the plan the word 'gold' has been omitted, but the yellow-leaved or yellow-variegated form of the shrub is always intended. There is a graceful cut-leaved golden elder that is desirable, as well as the common one.

Perhaps the Grey garden is seen at its best by reaching it through the orange borders. Here the eye becomes filled and saturated with the strong red and yellow colouring. This filling with the strong, rich colouring has the natural effect of making the eye eagerly desirous for the complementary colour, so that, standing by the inner yew arch and suddenly turning to look into the Grey garden, the effect is surprisingly – quite astonishingly – luminous and refeshing. One never knew before how vividly bright *Ageratum* could be, or lavender or *Nepeta* ; even the grey-purple of *Echinops* appears to have more positive colour than one's expectation would assign to it. The purple of the clematis of the Jackmanii group becomes piercingly brilliant, while the grey and glaucous foliage looks strangely cool and clear.

The plan shows the disposition of the plants, with grey-white edging of *Senecio cineraria*, *Stachys* and *Santolina*. There are groups of lavender with large-flowered clematis placed so that they may be trained close to them and partly over them. There are the monumental forms of the taller yuccas, *Y. gloriosa* and *Y. recurvifolia* towards the far angles, and, nearer the front (marked yucca in plan), the free-blooming *Y. filamentosa* of smaller size. The flower-colouring is of

Thalictrum, lupin and rue.

132

Lyme grass
(*Elymus arenarius*) and
soapwort (*Saponaria
officinalis*).

purple, pink and white. Besides the yuccas, the other white flowers are *Lilium longiflorum* and *L. candidum* (*L.c.* in plan), the clear white *Achillea* 'The Pearl' and the grey-white clouds of *Gypsophila paniculata*. The pink flowers are Sutton's *Godetia* 'Double Rose', sown in place early in May, the beautiful clear pink hollyhock 'Pink Beauty' and the pale pink double soapwort. *Clematis* 'Jackmanii' (*C.* in plan) and white everlasting pea are planted so that they can be trained to cover the gypsophila when its bloom is done and the seed-pods are turning brown. As soon as it loses its grey colouring the flowering tops are cut off, and the pea and clematis, already brought near, are trained over. When the gypsophila is making its strong growth in May, the shoots are regulated and supported by some stiff branching spray that is stuck among it. A little later this is quite hidden, but it remains as a firm substructure when the top of the gypsophila is cut back and the other plants are brought over.

Elymus is the blue-green lyme-grass, a garden form of the handsome blue-leaved grass that grows on the seaward edges of many of our sea-shore sandhills. The soapwort next to it is the double form of *Saponaria officinalis*, found wild in many places.

Of *Ageratum* two kinds are used – a brightly coloured one of the dwarf kinds for places near the front, where it tells as a close mass of colour, and the tall *A. houstonianum* for filling up further back in the border, where it shows as a diffuse purple cloud. The nepeta is the good garden catmint (*N. mussinii*). Its normal flowering-time is June, but it is cut half back, removing the first bloom, by the middle of the month, when it at once makes new flowering shoots.

Now, after the grey plants, the Gold garden looks extremely bright and sunny. A few minutes suffice to fill the eye with the yellow influence, and then we pass to the Blue garden, where there is another delightful shock of eye-pleasure. The brilliancy and purity of colour are almost incredible. Surely no blue flowers were ever so blue before! That is the impression received. For one thing, all the blue flowers used, with the exception of *Eryngium* and *Clematis heracleifolia* var. *davidiana*, are quite pure blues; these two are grey-blues. There are no purple-blues, such as the bluest of the campanulas and the perennial lupins; they would not be admissible. With the blues are a few white and palest yellow flowers; the foam-white *Clematis recta*, a delightful foil to Belladonna delphiniums; white perennial lupin with an almond-like softness of white; *Aruncus sylvester*, another foam-coloured flower. Then milk-white tree lupin, in its carefully decreed place near the bluish foliage of rue and yucca. Then there is the tender citron of lupin

(Far left) *Allium giganteum*, lamium, white lychnis and a low hedge of artemisia – a delightful beginning of a grey garden.

Delphinium and miscanthus.

135

The Green garden

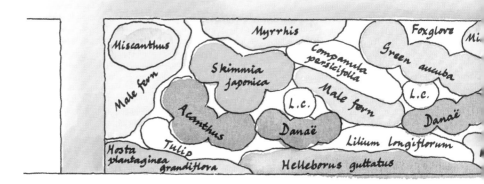

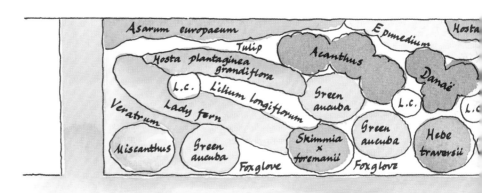

'Somerset' and the full canary of the tall yellow snapdragon, the diffused pale yellow of the soft plumy thalictrum and the strong canary of *Lilium szovitsianum*, with white everlasting pea and white Antwerp hollyhock at the back. White-striped maize grows up to cover the space left empty by the delphiniums when their bloom is over, and pots of *Plumbago capense* are dropped in to fill empty spaces. One group of this is trained over the bluish-leaved *Clematis recta*, which goes out of flower with the third week of July.

Yuccas, both of the large and small kinds, are also used in the Blue garden, and white lilies (*L. candidum* and *L. longiflorum*). There is foliage both of glaucous and of bright green colour, besides an

136

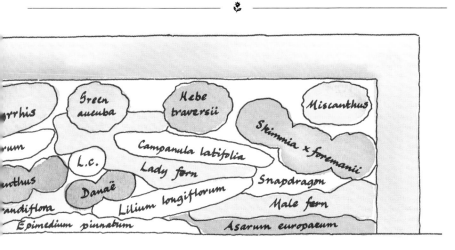

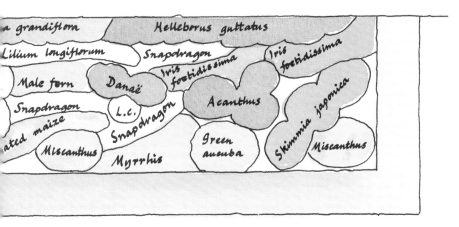

occasional patch of the silvery *Eryngium giganteum*. At the front edge are the two best hostas, *Hosta plantaginea* var. *grandiflora*, with leaves of bright yellow-green, and *H. sieboldiana*, whose leaves are glaucous. The variegated coltsfoot is a valuable edge-plant where the yellowish white of its bold parti-colouring is in place, and I find good use for the variegated form of the handsome grass *Glyceria aquatica*. Though this is a plant whose proper place is in wet ground, it will accommodate itself to the flower border, but it is well to keep it on the side away from the sun. It harmonizes well in colour with the coltsfoot; as a garden plant it is of the same class as the old ribbon grass, but is very much better. It is a good plan to replant it late in spring in order to

(Page 138) Grasses, sedges, bamboo, ferns and *Lysichitum* with the feathery plumes of *Aruncus sylvester* epitomize the cool refreshment of the Green garden.

(Page 139) Right to left: *Miscanthus sinensis* 'Zebrinus', *Ruscus aculeatus* and *Aucuba japonica*.

137

give it a check; if this is not done it has a rather worn-out appearance before the end of the summer; but if it is replanted or divided late in April it stands well throughout the season. The great white-striped Japanese grass, *Miscanthus sinensis* var. *variegatus*, is planted behind the delphiniums at the angles, and groups well with the maize.

From the Blue garden, passing eastward, we come to the Green garden. Shrubs of bright and deep green colouring and polished leaf-surface predominate. Here are green aucubas and skimmias, with *Danaë racemosa*, the beautiful Alexandrian or victory laurel, and more polished foliage of *Acanthus*, *Hosta*, *Asarum*, *Lilium candidum* and *L. longiflorum*, and *Iris fœtidissima*. Then feathery masses of paler green, male fern and lady fern and *Myrrhis odorata*, the handsome fern-like sweet Cicely of old English gardens. In the angles are again *Miscanthus sinensis* 'Zebrinus' – the variety with the leaves barred across with yellow.

In the Green garden the flowers are fewer and nearly all white – *Campanula latifolia* var. *alba* and *C. persicifolia*, lilies, tulips, foxgloves, snapdragons, peonies, hellebores – giving just a little bloom for each season to accompany the general scheme of polished and fern-like foliage. A little bloom of palest yellow shows in the front in May and June, with the flowers of *Uvularia* and *Epimedium*. But the Green garden, for proper development, should be on a much larger scale.

139

Chapter XIII

CLIMBING PLANTS

HEN one sees climbing plants or any of the shrubs that are so often used as climbers, planted in the usual way on a house or wall, about four feet apart and with no attempt at arrangement, it gives one that feeling of regret for opportunities lost or misused which is the sentiment most often aroused in the mind of the garden critic in the great number of pleasure-grounds that are planted without thought or discernment. Not infrequently in passing along a country road, with eye alert to note the beauties that are so often presented by little wayside cottage gardens, something is seen that may well serve as a lesson in better planting. The lesson is generally one that teaches greater simplicity – the doing of one thing at a time; the avoidance of overmuch detail. One such cottage has under the parlour window an old bush of *Chaenomeles japonica*. It had been kept well spurred back and must have been a mass of gorgeous bloom in early spring. The rest of the cottage was embowered in an old grape vine, perhaps of all wall plants the most beautiful, and, I always think, the most harmonious with cottages or small houses of the cottage class. It would seem to be least in place on the walls of houses of classical type; indeed, such houses are often better without any wall-plants. Still, there are occasions where the noble polished foliage of magnolia comes admirably on their larger spaces, and the clear-cut refinement of myrtle on their lesser areas of wall-surface.

It is, like all other matters of garden planning, a question of knowledge and good taste. The kind of wall or house and its neighbouring forms are taken into account and a careful choice is made of the most suitable plants. For my own part I like to give a house, whatever its size or style, some dominant note in wall-planting. In my own home, which is a house of the large cottage class, the prevailing wall-growths are vines and figs in the south and west, and in a shady northward-facing court between two projecting wings, *Clematis montana* on the two cooler sides, and again a vine upon the other. At

Top: *Clematis flammula*; side, *Solanum crispum*.

140

one angle on the warmer side of the house, where the height to the
eaves is not great, China roses have been trained up, and rosemary,
which clothes the whole foot of the wall, is here encouraged to rise
with them. The colour of the China rose bloom and the dusky green of
the rosemary are always to me one of the most charming combinations.
In remembrance of the cottage example lately quoted there is *Chaenomeles japonica* under the long sitting-room window. I remember
another cottage that had a porch covered with the golden balls of
Kerria japonica, and China roses reaching up the greater part of the low
walls of half timber and plastering; the pink roses seeming to ask one
which of them were the loveliest in colour; whether it was those that
came against the silvery-grey of the old oak or those that rested on the
warm-white plaster. It should be remembered that of all roses the pink
China is the one that is more constantly in bloom than any other, for
its first flowers are perfected before the end of May, and in sheltered
places the later ones last till Christmas.

The *Clematis montana* in the court riots over the wall facing east and
up over the edge of the roof. At least it appears to riot, but is really
trained and regulated; the training favouring its natural way of
throwing down streamers and garlands of its long bloom-laden cordage. At one point it runs through and over a guelder rose that is its
only wall companion. Then it turns to the left and is trained in garlands along a moulded oak beam that forms the base of a timbered
wall with plastered panels.

But this is only one way of using this lovely climbing plant. Placed
at the foot of any ragged tree – old worn-out apple or branching thorn

Clematis montana
'Tetrarose' drapes a wall
with its dusky pink
flowers. The subdued
colouring is picked up
by the leaves of purple
sage, grey mounds of
catmint and the flowers
of a perennial
wallflower.

— or a rough brake of bramble and other wild bushes, it will soon fill or cover it with its graceful growth and bounteous bloom. It will rush up a tall holly or clothe an old hedgerow where thorns have run up and become thin and gappy, or cover any unsightly sheds or any kind of outbuilding. All clematis prefer a chalky soil, but *C. montana* does not insist on this, and in my garden they are growing in sandy ground. In the end of May it comes into bloom, and is at its best in the early days of June. When the flowers are going over and the white petals show that slightly shrivelled surface that comes before they fall, they give off a sweet scent like vanilla. This cannot always be smelt from the actual flowers, but is carried by the air blowing over the flowering mass; it is a thing that is often a puzzle to owners of gardens some time in the second week of June.

Another of these clematis, which, like *Clematis montana* of gardens, is very near the wild species and is good for all the same purposes, is *C. flammula*, blooming in September. Very slightly trained it takes the form of flowery clouds. It can be used in various ways, on a cottage, on an oak-paled fence and on a wall combined with the feathery foliage of *Sorbaria tomentosa*. I do not think there is any incident in my garden that has been more favourably noticed than the happy growth of these two plants together. The wall faces north a little west, and every year it is a delight to see not only the beauty of associated form, but the loveliness of the colouring; for the clematis bloom has the warm white of foam and the sorbaria has leaves of the rather pale green of lady fern, besides a graceful fern-like form and a slight twist or turn also of a fern-like character. But this clematis has many other uses, for bowers, arches and pergolas, as well as for many varied aspects of wild gardening.

A shrub for wall use that is much neglected, though of the highest beauty, is *Abutilon vitifolium*. In our northern and midland counties it may not be hardy, but it does well anywhere south of London. The flowers, each two and a half inches across, are borne in large, loose clusters, their tender lavender colour harmonizing perfectly with the greyish, downy foliage.

There is no lovelier or purer blue than that of the newly opened *Ipomoea tricolor*, popularly known as 'Heavenly Blue', and well deserving the name. It must be raised in heat early in the year and be put out in June against a warm wall. Here it is in a narrow border at the

142

foot of a wall facing south-west, where, by the aid of a few short pea-sticks, it climbs into the lower branches of a vine. The vine is one of the Chasselas kind, with leaves of a rather pale green, almost yellowish-green colouring that makes the best possible foil to the pure blue of the ipomoea. To my eye it is the most enjoyable colour-feast of the year.

Solanum crispum, with purple flowers in goodly bunches, is one of the best of wall shrubs. Another of the tender plants that is beautiful for walls and for free rambling over other wall-growths is *S. jasminoides*. Its white clusters come into bloom in middle summer and persist till latest autumn. In two gardens near me it is of singular beauty ; in the one case on the sunny wall of a sheltered court where it covers a considerable space, in the other against a high south retaining-wall where, from the terrace above, the flowers are seen against the misty woodland of the middle distance and the pure grey-blue of the far-away hills. Turning round on the very same spot, there is the remarkable growth of *Lippia citriodora*, or lemon-scented verbena, that owes its luxuriance to its roots and main shoots being under shelter. There must be unending opportunities, where there are verandahs, of having just such bowers of sweetness to brush against in passing and to waft scented air to the windows of the rooms above.

These notes can only touch upon the more careful use of a few of the many climbing plants and trailing shrubs. One of the many garden possessions that I ardently desire and can never have is a bit of rocky hill-side ; a place partly of sheer scarp and partly of tumbled and out-cropping rock-mass, for the best use of these plants. There would be

(Far left) Morning glory (*Ipomoea*) and yellow-green grape leaves.

'One is always watching and trying for good combinations of colour'. *Rosa* 'New Dawn' and *Clematis* 'Perle d'Azur' is a perfect combination for a stone wall.

the place for the yellow winter jasmine (*Jasminum nudiflorum*), for the honeysuckles both bushy and rambling, for the trailing clematis lately described and for the native *C. vitalba*, beautiful both in flower and fruit; for shrubs like *Forsythia suspensa* and *Lespedeza thunbergii*, that like to root high and then throw down cascades of bloom, and for the wichuraiana roses, also for gourds and wild vines. There should be a good quarter of a mile of it so that one might plant at perfect ease, one thing at a time or one or two in combination, in just such sized and shaped groups as would make the most delightful pictures, and in just the association that would show the best assortment.

I have seen long stretches of bare chalky banks for year after year with nothing done to dispel their bald monotony, feeling inward regret at the wasted opportunity; thinking how beautiful they might be made with a planting of two common things, *Clematis vitalba* and red spur valerian. But such examples are without end.

145

Chapter XIV

GROUPINGS OF PLANTS
IN POTS

IT is a common thing in Italian gardens to see a quantity of plants in pots standing in various parts of the garden, generally in connection with paved terraces and steps. This is in addition to the larger pot plants – oranges, lemons, oleanders, &c. – that, in their immense and often richly decorated earthenware receptacles, form an important part of the garden design. In our climate we cannot have these unless there is an orangery or some such spacious place free from frost for housing them in winter. But good groupings of smaller plants in pots is a form of ornament that might be made more use of in our own gardens, especially where there are paved spaces near a house or in connection with a tank or fountain, so that there is convenient access to means of daily watering. I have such a space in a cool court nearly square in shape. A middle circle is paved, and all next the house is paved, on a level of one shallow step higher. It is on the sides of this raised step that the pot plants are grouped, leaving free access to a wooden seat in the middle, and a clear way to a door on the left.

The first thing is to secure good greenery. On each side three oblong Italian terra-cotta pots full of *Hosta plantaginea* var. *grandiflora* stand on the lower level. They serve to hide the common flower-pots that are ranged behind. The pots are arranged early in June when the *Clematis montana* is still in bloom. Next above the ornamental pots are common ones, also with the same hostas. On the inner side of the groups, next the house, are pots of aspidistra, and, against the wall, of male fern, and there are more ferns and hostas for filling spaces between the flowering plants. Of these the most important are lilies – *L. longiflorum*, *L. candidum* and *L. speciosum* – and hydrangeas, but we also have pots of Spanish irises, of *Gladiolus nanus* 'The Bride', *Campanula persicifolia* and *C. pyramidalis*, of white and pink phloxes and of white and pink cup-and-saucer Canterbury bells. The last are taken up from the ground and potted only just before they come into bloom.

There are seldom more than two kinds of flowering plants placed here at a time; the two or three sorts of beautiful foliage are in themselves delightful to the eye; often there is nothing with them but lilies, and one hardly desires to have more. There is an ample filling of the green plants, so that no pots are seen.

If the place were in the sun the plants chosen would be largely geraniums (*Pelargonium*); two-year-old plants in good-sized pots; and, in place of the ferns that enjoy shade and the hostas whose leaves often burn in the sun, there would be the large-leaved *Bergenia cordifolia*. Here also would be lilies, hydrangeas and cannas, and good store of the graceful maiden's wreath (*Francoa ramosa*).

The geraniums would be very carefully assorted for colour; in one part of the scheme white and soft pink, in another the rosy scarlets, and elsewhere the salmon-reds, now so numerous and good. The last two groups might by degrees tone into the pure scarlets, of which the best I know and the most delightful in colour is 'Paul Crampel'. The colour is pure and brilliant but not *cruel*.

I have great pleasure in putting together 'Omphale', palest salmon-pink; 'Mrs Laurence', a shade deeper; 'Mrs Cannell', a salmon-scarlet,

Left to right: *Hosta plantaginea* (leaf and flower spike), *Aspidistra lurida* and male fern (*Dryopteris filix-mas*).

147

Of flowering plants in pots for the north court of Munstead Wood, 'often there is nothing . . . . but lilies, and one hardly desires to have more'. Lilies flourish in pots, where the soil can be varied to suit their individual requirements and their refinement and perfume can be enjoyed to the full.

and leading these by degrees to the pure, good scarlet of 'Paul Crampel'. A bed or clump or border planted with these, or varieties equivalent in colour, would be seen to have a quite remarkable degree of life, brilliancy, beauty and interest.

For detached vases that stand on pedestals, so that the whole of the vase and contents becomes warmed by exposure to sunlight, a condition specially grateful to geraniums, I know no variety more useful than 'King of Denmark'. The flowers are in large trusses, half-double, of an excellent soft salmon-pink colour; the foliage is bold and well marked; the whole plant massive and handsome. For this and any other outdoor pot-culture it is best if strong two-year-old plants can be kept.

There are among geraniums some of a raw magenta-pink that I re-gret to see in many gardens and that will certainly never be admitted into mine.

In designing gardens where there are flagged spaces it is well to remember the good effect of summer flowers in slightly raised beds with stone edges. Such beds often come happily in conjunction with steps and paved landings and designs in which fountains occur. Sum-mer flowers, such as geraniums, lilies and cannas, seem to revel in such beds and are never seen to better advantage. Owing to the cottage character of my house I have little scope for such beds – none at all for the best kind with dwarf walls and kerbs of moulded freestone, but I have one edged with a low wall of local sandstone where there is a square landing paved with the same stone and short flights of steps in connection with a tank and a lower garden level. Here geraniums and cannas luxuriate in shelter and full sunshine.

Maiden's wreath (*Francoa ramosa*) is a plant for many uses. The foliage, though sparing in quantity, is distinct and handsome. The long flower-stems are flung out with a kind of determination of character that would seem to imply that the plant knows what is ex-pected of it and intends to fulfil its settled duty and purpose, namely, that of being a graceful and beautiful ornament. Towards the later summer these flower-stems become so heavy that there is danger of their weight, swayed by a little wind, wrenching out whole portions of the plant. Support should be given with short pieces of hazel stick tied half way up the stem. In nurseries it is general, and even in private gardens not unusual, to see the flowers tied straight upright. This

148

should never be, for it not only forces the plant into a form that is entirely at variance with its nature, but robs it of its natural grace and valuable individuality.

There is no end to the uses of hydrangeas in pots ; a well-bloomed plant will give life and interest to many an uninteresting corner ; the bloom is long-enduring and stands equally well in sun and shade. If the blue colour, which comes naturally in some soils, is desired, it can be had by mixing pounded slate and iron filings with the compost — alum is another well-known agent for inducing the blue colour. But I have much faith in slate, for the bluest I have ever seen came from a garden on a slaty soil.

A few only of the many plants that can with advantage be used in pots have been named, but in any case it would be well to bear in mind that it is best to restrict the number of kinds shown at once and to make sure of the good groundwork of foliage. I have therefore only dwelt upon the few that came to mind as the best and easiest to use. But the pretty red and white single fuchsias of the 'Mme Cornelissen' type should not be forgotten ; and the fine Comet and Ostrich Plume asters are capital pot-plants, for, like Canterbury bells, they bear lifting from the open ground just before they flower and even in full bloom.

Geraniums and cannas in a stone-edged bed.

150

Plants grown in pots lead naturally to the consideration of those most suitable for tubs. Of these the most important are permanent things of shrubby nature – several of the orange and lemon family, oleander, pomegranate, bay, myrtle, *Datura*, sweet verbena and dwarf palm, also hydrangea, tree heliotrope and *Agapanthus*. The last is of course a bulbous plant, but from its large, solid foliage and quantity of long-enduring bloom it is one of the best of plants for tubs. The greater number of these need housing in winter in an orangery or other frost-proof building. Other bushy plants for tub use that are hardier are some of the hebes such as *HH. brachysiphon, speciosa* and *hulkeana*, *Olearia haastii* and *O.* 'Scilloniensis'. Tree peonies, though rarely so used, are capital tub plants, and, though they are not very long in flower, their supreme beauty makes them desirable. They should certainly be grown in places where labour is not restricted and where there are suitable places for standing such plants away and caring for them in the off season.

For the same kind of use the tree lupins, both white and yellow, would be excellent. *Hosta sieboldiana* also makes a handsome tub, while

Yellow canna and lemon-scented *Lippia citriodora*.

151

for summer filling cannas are admirable and old geraniums in bush form always acceptable. I have never seen *Acanthus* used in this way, but can see no reason against it. The smaller bamboos, such as the handsome broad-leaved *Sasa tessellata*, are very good in tubs. In speaking of plants suitable for tubs, I take the word to include the larger sizes of terra-cotta pots; but *Agapanthus* should never be planted in earthenware, as the roots, which remain for many years undisturbed, have so strong a rending power that they will burst anything less resisting than iron-hooped wood.

It is rare to see, anywhere in England, plant-tubs painted a pleasant colour. In nearly every garden they are painted a strong raw green with the hoops black, whereas any green that is not bright and raw would be much better. This matter of the colouring of all such garden accessories as have to be painted deserves more attention than it commonly receives. Doors in garden walls, trellises, wooden railings and hand-gates and seats – all these and any other items of woodwork that stand out in the garden and are seen among its flowers and foliage should, if painted green, be of such a green as does not for brightness come into competition with the green of leaves. In the case of tubs especially, it is the plant that is to be considered first – not the tub. The bright, harsh green on the woodwork makes the colour of the foliage look dull and ineffective. It would be desirable, in the case of solitary tub plants, to study the exact colour that would be most becoming to the flower and foliage; but as it is needful, to avoid a patchy appearance, to paint the whole of the tubs in any one garden scheme the same colour, a tint should be chosen that is quiet in itself and that is lower in tone than the dullest of the foliage in any of the examples. Moreover, there is no reason for painting the hoops black; it is much better to paint the whole out of one pot.

A good quiet green can be made with black, chrome No.1 and white lead, enough white being mixed to give the depth or lightness desired.

Elsewhere I have written of the deplorable effect in the garden landscape of the glaring white paint – still worse when tinted blue – that emphasizes the ugliness of the usual greenhouse or conservatory. This may be mitigated, if the unsightly structure cannot be concealed, by adding to the white a good deal of black and raw umber, till the paint is of the quiet warm grey that for some strange reason is known to house-painters as Portland-stone colour.

Top: *Acanthus spinosus*; bottom: *Hosta sieboldiana*.

152

Chapter XV

SOME GARDEN PICTURES

WHEN the eye is trained to perceive pictorial effect, it is frequently struck by something – some combination of grouping, lighting and colour – that is seen to have that complete aspect of unity and beauty that to the artist's eye forms a picture. Such are the impressions that the artist-gardener endeavours to produce in every portion of the garden. Many of these good intentions fail, some come fairly well; a few reward him by a success that was beyond anticipation. When this is the case it is probably due to some cause that had been overlooked but that had chanced to complete his intention, such as the position of the sun in relation to some wished-for colour-picture. Then there are some days during the summer when the quality of light seems to tend to an extraordinary beauty of effect. I have never been able to find out how the light on these occasions differs from that of ordinary fine summer days, but, when these days come, I know them and am filled with gladness.

In the case of my own garden, so far, as deliberate intention goes, what is aimed at is something quite simple and devoid of complication; generally one thing or a very limited number of flowering things at a time, but that one, or those few things, carefully placed so as to avoid fuss, and give pleasure to the eye and ease to the mind. In many cases the aim has been to show some delightful colour combination without regard to the other considerations that go to the making of a more ambitious picture. It may be a group in a shrub border, or a combination of border and climbing plants, or some carefully designed company of plants in the rock garden. I have a little rose that I call the Fairy Rose. It came to me from a cottage garden, and I have never seen it elsewhere. It grows about a foot high and has blush-pink flowers with the colour deepening to the centre. In character the flower is somewhere between the lovely 'Blush Boursault' at its best and the

little 'De Meaux'. It is an inch and a half across and of beautiful form, especially in the half-opened bud. Wishing to enjoy its beauty to the utmost, and to bring it comfortably within sight, I gave it a shelf in raised rock-work and brought near and under it a clear pale lilac viola and a good drift of *Achillea umbellata*. It was worth doing. Another combination that gives me much pleasure is that of the pink pompon rose 'Cameo' with catmint and whitish foliage, such as *Stachys* or *Artemisia stelleriana*. I may have mentioned this before, but it is so pretty that it deserves repetition.

In a shrubbery border the fine *Aruncus sylvester* is beautiful with an interplanting of *Thalictrum aquilegifolium* var. *atropurpureum*. At the end of a long flower-clump there is a yew hedge coming forward at right angles to the length of the border. Behind the hedge is a stone wall with an arch, through which the path in front of the border passes. Over the stone arch, and rambling partly over the yews, are the vigorous many-flowered growths of *Clematis flammula*. At the end of the border are pale sulphur-coloured Antwerp hollyhocks. Both in form and colour this was a delightful picture; the foam-like masses of the clematis resting on the dusky richness of the yew; the straight shafts of the Antwerp hollyhock giving clear colour and agreeing with the upright lines of the sides of the archway, which showed dimly in the shade. These are only a few incidents out of numbers that occur or are intentionally arranged.

Whether the arrangement is simple and modest, obvious or subtle 'the aim is always to use the plants to the best of one's means and intelligence'. Here subtlety succeeds: Indigofera, lilies, roses and *Campanula lactiflora* create a soft blend of colours 'all a little sad'.

155

An incident on the steps: allowing plants to seed into cracks links steps with their surroundings and, carefully fostered, provides a series of garden pictures in miniature.

There is a place near my house where a path leads down through a nut-walk to the further garden. It is crossed by a shorter path that ends at a birch-tree with a tall silvered trunk. It seemed desirable to accentuate the point where the paths cross; I therefore put down four square platforms of stone 'pitching' as a place for the standing of four hydrangeas in tubs. Just before the tree is a solid wooden seat and a shallow wide step done with the same stone pitching. Tree and seat are surrounded on three sides by a rectangular planting of yews. The tender greys of the rugged lower bark of the birch and the silvering of its upper stem tell finely against the dark velvet-like richness of the yew and the leaf-mass of other trees beyond; the pink flowers and fresh green foliage of the hydrangeas are also brilliant against the dusky green. It is just one simple picture that makes one glad for three months of the later summer and early autumn. The longer cross-path, which on the right leads in a few yards to steps up to the paved court on the north side of the house, on the left passes down the nut-walk. The birch-tree and seat are immediately to the right, just out of the picture. Standing a little way down the shaded nut-walk and looking back, the hydrangeas are seen in another aspect, with the steps and house behind them in shade, and the sun shining through their pale green leaves. Sitting on the seat, the eye, passing between the pink hydrangea flowers, sees a short straight path bounded by a wall of tree box to right and left, and at the far end one tub of pale blue hydrangea in shade, backed by a repetition of the screen of yews such as enclose the birch-tree.

On the south side of the house there is a narrow border full of rosemary, with China roses and a vine. Here the narrow lawn, backed by woodland, is higher than the house-level. Shallow steps lead up to it in the middle, and to right and left is low dry-walling. On the upper edge of this is a hedge of Burnet roses, and in the narrow border below, a planting of the low-growing *Leucothoë axillaris*, a little shrub that is neat throughout the year and in winter prettily red-tinted.

The beautiful white lily cannot be grown in the hot sandy soil of my garden. Even if its place be ever so well prepared with the loam and lime that it loves, the surrounding soil-influences seems to rob it of its needful nourishment; it makes a miserable show for one year and never appears again. The only way to grow it is in pots or tubs sunk in the soil. For some years I had wished to have an orderly planting of this

156

lovely lily in the lower border at the back of the *Leucothoë* just in front of the Burnet roses. I had no flower-pots deep enough, or wide enough at the bottom, but was able to make a contrivance with some short, broad, unglazed drain-pipes, measuring a foot long and of about the same diameter, by cementing in an artificial bottom made of pieces of roofing-tile and broken flower-pot, leaving spaces for drainage. Then three bulbs were put in each pot in a compost that I knew they would enjoy. When they were half grown the pots were sunk in holes at nearly even distances among the leucothoës, and in few weeks my row of lilies gave me my reward. Other lilies (*L. longiflorum*) follow them a month later, just beyond in the wood edge among tufts of male fern, and a pot of *Francoa* is to right and left of the shallow steps.

During the last year or two some pretty incidents have occurred about these same steps ; not important enough to call garden pictures, but charming and interesting and easily enjoyable because they are close to the open garden door of the sitting-room and because they teach me to look out for the desirable things that come of themselves. A seedling of the wild clematis (*C. vitalba*) appeared among the briars to the left. As it was too strong a plant to let grow over them un-checked, I pulled it forward towards the steps, training one or two shoots to run along the hollow of the step and laying on them pieces of stone, invisible among the foliage, to keep them from being dislodged by the skirts of visitors or the gambols of my cats. At the same time, in a crack of the stone just below the upper step there came a seedling of the tall chimney campanula (*C. pyramidalis*). The second year this threw up its tall flower-stem and was well in bloom when it was wrecked by an early autumn gale, the wind wrenching out the crown and upper root-stock. But a little shred of rooted life remained, and now there is again the sturdy tuft promising more flower-stems for the coming season.

Close behind the bell-flower a spreading sheet of wild thyme has crept out of the turf and flowed rather widely over the stone. Luckily I just saved it from the tidying process that threatened it, and as it is now well established over the stone I still have the pleasure of its bright rosy bloom when the duties of the mowing-machine rob me of the other tiny flowers – hawkweed, milkwort and bedstraw – that bloom so bravely in the intervals between its ruthless but indispens-able ministrations.

Chapter XVI

A BEAUTIFUL FRUIT
GARDEN

THERE is a whole range of possible beautiful treatment in fruit-growing that is rarely carried out or even attempted. Hitherto but little has been done to make the fruit garden a place of beauty; we find it almost flaunting its unloveliness, its white painted orchard-houses and vineries, its wires and wire-nettings. It is not to be denied that all these are necessary, and that the usual and most obvious way of working them does not make for beauty. But in designing new gardens or remodelling old, on a rather large scale, there need be no difficulty in so arranging that all that is necessarily unbeautiful should be kept in one department, so hedged or walled around as to be out of sight.

In addition to such a fruit garden for strict utility I have in mind a walled enclosure of about an acre and a half, longer than wide. I have seen in large places just such spaces, actually walled but put to no use.

The wall has trained fruit-trees – peaches spreading their goodly fans, pears showing long, level lines, and including hardy grape vines, giving all the best exposition of the hardy fruit-grower's art. Next to the wall is a space six feet wide for ample access to the fruit-trees, their pruning, training and root-management; then a fourteen-foot plant border, wholly for beauty, and a path eight feet wide. At a middle point on all four sides the high wall has an arched doorway corresponding to the grassy way between the fruit-trees in the middle space. If the wall has some symmetrical building on the outside of each angle, so much the better; the garden can make use of all. One may be a bothy, with lower extension out of sight; one a half-underground fruit-store, with bulb-store above; a third a paint-shop, and a fourth a tea-house.

The middle space is all turf; in the centre a mulberry, and, both ways across, double lines of fruit-trees, ending with bays. In almost

159

any part of the sea-warmed south of England, below the fifty-first parallel of latitude, which passes throught the upper part of Sussex, the rows of fruit-trees on the green might be standard figs; elsewhere they would be bush pears and apples. If the soil is calcareous, so much the better for the figs and mulberry, the vines and indeed nearly all the fruits. The angle-clumps in the grass are planted with magnolias, yuccas and hydrangeas.

The border all round is for small shrubs and plants of some solidity or importance; the spaces are too long for an ordinary flower border. It would have a good bush of *Magnolia stellata* at each angle, yuccas, kniphofias, hardy fuchsias, peonies, *Euphorbia wulfenii*, hollyhocks, dahlias, hydrangeas, Michaelmas daisies, flag iris, the beautiful *Olearia* 'Scilloniensis' and *O. haastii*, tree lupins, forsythia, weigela, the smaller bush spiraeas, hebes, tamarisk, the large-bloomed kinds of clematis, bush kinds of garden roses, hostas, and so on.

Surely my fruit garden would be not only a place of beauty, of pleasant sight and pleasant thought, but of leisurely repose, a repose broken only faintly and in welcome fashion by its own interests – in July, August and September a goodly place in which to wander and find luscious fruits in quantity that can be gathered and eaten straight

Pears, mulberries and peach.

160

'Surely my fruit garden would be not only a place of beauty . . . but of leisurely repose . . . a good place to wander and find luscious fruits. How delicious are the sun-warmed apricots'.

from the tree. There is a pleasure in searching for and eating fruit in this way that is far better than having it picked by the gardener and brought in and set before one on a dish in a tame room. Is this feeling an echo of far-away days of savagery when men hunted for their food and rejoiced to find it, or is it rather the poet's delight of having direct intercourse with the good gift of the growing thing and seeing and feeling through all the senses how good and gracious the thing is? To pass the hand among the leaves of the fig-tree, noting that they are a little harsh upon the upper surface and yet soft beneath; to be aware of their faint, dusky scent; to see the cracking of the coat of the fruit and the yellowing of the neck where it joins the branch – the two indi-cations of ripeness – sometimes made clearer by the drop of honeyed moisture at the eye; then the handling of the fruit itself, which must needs be gentle because the tender coat is so readily bruised and torn; at the same time observing the slight greyish bloom and the colouring – low-toned transitions of purple and green; and finally to have the enjoyment of the luscious pulp, with the knowledge that it is one of the most wholesome and sustaining of fruit foods – surely all this is worthy garden service! Then how delicious are the sun-warmed apricots and peaches, and, later in the year, the Jargonelle pears,

(Page 162) 'What is more lovely than the bloom of orchard trees in April and May with the grass below in its strong young growth'. Here the cowslips have hybridized with red bunch-flowered primroses, producing varied hues of red, soft orange and pale yellow to enhance the spring scene.

always best eaten straight from the tree; and the ripe mulberries of September. And how pleasant to stroll about the wide grassy ways, turning from the fruits to the flowers in the clumps and borders; to the splendid yuccas and the masses of hydrangea bloom, and then to the gorgeous kniphofias and other delights; and to see the dignity of the stately bay-trees and the incomparable beauty of their every twig and leaf.

The beautiful fruit garden would naturally lead to the orchard, a place that is not so often included in the pleasure-ground as it deserves. For what is more lovely than the bloom of orchard trees in April and May, with the grass below in its strong, young growth; in itself a garden of cowslips and daffodils. In an old orchard how pictorial are the lines of the low-leaning old apple-trunks and the swing and poise of their upper branches, best seen in winter when their graceful movement of line and wonderful sense of balance can be fully appreciated. But the younger orchard has its beauty too, of fresh, young life and wealth of bloom and bounteous bearing.

Then if the place of the orchard suggests a return to nearer pleasure-ground with yet some space between, how good to make this into a free garden orchard for the fruits of wilder character; for wide-spreading medlars, for quinces, again some of the most graceful of small British trees; for service, damson, bullace, crabs and their many allies, not fruit-bearing trees except from the birds' and botanists' points of view, but beautiful both in bloom and berry, such as the mountain ash, wild cherry, blackthorn, and the large-berried white-thorns, bird-cherry, whitebeam, holly and amelanchier. Then all these might be intergrouped with great brakes of the free-growing roses and the wilder kinds of clematis and honeysuckle. And right through it should be a shady path of filberts or cobnuts arching overhead and yielding a grateful summer shade and a bountiful autumn harvest.

Crab apple (*Malus floribunda*) and honeysuckle (*Lonicera periclymenum*).

163

Chapter XVII

PLANTING FOR WINTER COLOUR

MUCH cheerful positive colour, other than that given by flowers or leaves, may be obtained in winter by using a good selection of small trees with coloured bark. Of these the most useful are the red dogwood and some of the willows. This planting for colour of bright-barked trees is no new thing, for a good half century ago the late Lord Somers, at Eastnor Castle near Malvern, used to 'paint his woods', as he described it, in this way.

The cardinal willow has bright red bark, *Salix alba* 'Chermesina' orange, and the golden osier bright yellow. The yearly growth has the best-coloured bark, so that when they are employed for giving colour it is usual to cut them every winter; moreover, the large quantity of young shoots that the cutting induces naturally increases the density of the colour effect. But if they are planted in a rather large way it is better that the regular winter cutting should be restricted to those near the outer edge, and to let a good proportion of those within stand for two or more years, and to have some in the background that are never cut at all, but that are allowed to grow to their full size and to show their natural habit.

It will also be well, instead of planting them exclusively sort by sort, to group and intergroup carefully assorted colours, such as the scarlet willow with the purple-barked kind (*Salix daphnoides*) and to let this pass into the American willow with the black stem. Such a group should not be too large, and it should be near the pathway, for it will show best near at hand. For the sake of the bark-colouring, it would be best to cut it all every year, although in the larger plantings it is desirable to have the trees of different ages, or the effect may be too much that of a mere crop instead of a well-arranged garden grouping.

Some of the garden roses, both of the free-growing and bush kinds, have finely coloured bark that can be used in much the same way. They

Among plants with coloured bark, 'the most useful are the red dogwoods and some of the willows'. In this winter garden, red- and yellow-stemmed dogwoods arise among the cheering foliage of variegated *Euonymus fortunei*.

164

are specially good in broken ground, such as the banks of an old hollow cart-way converted to garden use, or the sloping *débris* of a quarry. Of the free kinds, the best coloured are *Rosa ferruginea*, whose leaves are red as well as the stem – it is the *R. rubrifolia* of nurseries[12] – and the varieties of Boursault roses, derived from *R. × reclinata*. As bushes for giving reddish colouring, *R. virginiana* would be among the best.

By waterside the great reedmace – commonly but wrongly called bulrush – holds its handsome seedheads nearly through the winter, and beds of the common reed (*Phragmites communis*) stand up the winter through in masses of light, warm colouring that are grateful to the eye and suggest comfortable harbourage for wildfowl.

Some shrubs have conspicuously green bark, such as the spindle-tree; but the habit of growth is rather too diffuse to let it make a distinct show of colour. *Leycesteria formosa* is being tried in mass for winter colour in some gardens, but I venture to feel a little doubtful of its success; for though the skin of the half-woody stem is bright green, the plant has the habit of retaining some of its leaves and the remains of its flowering tips till January, or even later. After frost these have the appearance of untidy grey rags, and are distinctly unsightly. The brightest effect of all green-barked plants is that given by whortle-berry, a plant that on peaty or sandy soils is one of the most enjoyable of winter undershrubs.

It would add greatly to the enjoyment of many country places if some portions were planted with evergreens expressly for winter effect. Some region on the outskirts of the garden, and between it and wood-land, would be the most desirable. If well done the sense of wintry discomfort would disappear, for nearly all the growing things would be at their best, and even in summer, shrubs and plants can do no more than this. In summer, too, it would be good to see, for the green things would have such an inter-planting of free roses, jasmines, *Clematis*, honeysuckles, *Forsythia*, and so on, as would make charming incidents of flower-beauty.

The place for this winter walk should be sheltered from the north and east. I have such a place in my mind's eye, where, beyond the home garden and partly wooded old shrubbery, there is a valley running up into a pine-wooded hill. The path goes up the hill-side diagonally, with a very gentle gradient. In the cooler, lower portion

The mysterious mistiness of winter, 'a beauty which no summer landscape can show' and a theme with which Miss Jekyll began and ended her book, is a salutary reminder of nature's contribution to the efforts of man in the garden.

there would be rhododendrons and kalmias, with lesser growths of *Skimmia* and *Gaultheria*. Close to the path, on the less sunny side, would be Lent hellebores and the delightful winter greenery of *Epimedium*. Then in full sun *Pieris japonica*, and on the shadier side *Pieris floribunda*. Both of these hard and rather brittle-wooded shrubs form dense bushes four or more feet high. At their foot would be the lower-growing leucothoës, with lissome branches of a more willow-like character. These make a handsome ground-carpeting from one to three feet high, beautiful at all seasons – the leaves in winter tinted or marbled with red. Portions of the cooler side would also have fringes of hartstongue and polypody, both winter ferns. Then, as the path rose into more direct sunlight, there would be cistuses – in all mild winter days giving off their strong, cordial scent – and the dwarf rhododendrons. Behind the cistuses would be white broom, finely green-stemmed in winter. There would even be shrubs in flower; the thick-set yellowish bloom of witch hazel (*Hamamelis*) and the bright yellow of *Jasminum nudiflorum*. Then groups of junipers, and all the ground carpeted with heath, and so to the upper pine-wood. Then, after the comforting greenery of the lower region, the lovely colour of distant winter landscape would be intensely enjoyable; for the greys and

Left to right: *Leucothoë fontanesiana*, *Skimmia japonica* and *Polypodium vulgare*.

purples of the leafless woodland of middle distance have a beauty that no summer landscape can show. In clear weather the further distances have tints of an extraordinary purity, while the more frequent days of slightly distant haze have another kind of beautiful mystery.

The common laurel is generally seen as a long-suffering garden hack, put to all sorts of rather ignoble uses. It is so cheap to buy, so quick of growth and so useful as an easily made screen that its better use is, except in rare instances, lost sight of. Planted in thin woodland and never pruned, it grows into a small tree that takes curious ways and shapes of trunk and branch of a character that is remarkably pictorial.

Chapter XVIII

FORM IN PLANTING

I F in the foregoing chapters I have dwelt rather insistently on matters of colour, it is not that I under-rate the equal importance of form and proportion, but that I think that the question of colour, as regards its more careful use, is either more commonly neglected or has had fewer exponents. As in all matters relating to design in gardening, the good placing of plants in detail is a matter of knowledge of an artistic character. The shaping of every group of plants, to have the best effect, should not only be definitely intended, but should be done with an absolute conviction by the hand that feels the *drawing* that the group must have in relation what is near, or to the whole form of the clump or border or whatever the nature of the place may be. I am only too well aware that to many this statement may convey no idea whatever; nevertheless I venture to insist upon its truth. Moreover, I am addressing this book to the consideration of those who are in sympathy with my views of gardening, among whom I know there are many who, even if they have not made themselves able, by study and long practice, to show in groundwork and garden design the quality known to artists as *drawing* – by which is meant a right movement of line and form and group – can at least recognize its value – indeed, its supreme importance – when it is present, and do not, in its absence, fail to feel that the thing shown is without life, spirit, or reasonable justification.

Even a proficiency in some branch of fine art does not necessarily imply ability to lay out ground. I have known, in the intimate association of half a lifetime, a landscape painter whose interpretation of natural beauty was of the most refined and poetical quality, and who truly loved flowers and beautiful vegetation, but who was quite incapable of personally arranging a garden; although it is more usual that an artist should almost unconsciously place plants well.

It is therefore not to be expected that it is enough to buy good plants and merely to tell the gardener of average ability to plant them

169

Form in planting.
(Two plans of a
heath garden)

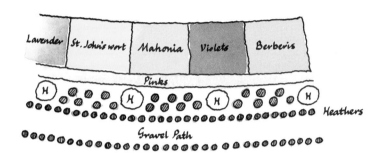

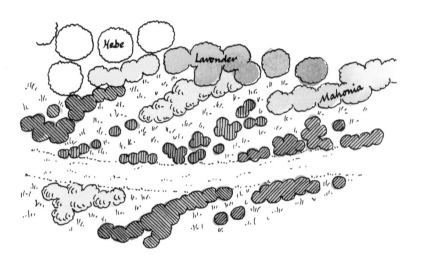

in groups, as is now often done with the very best intention. It is impossible for the gardener to know what is meant. In all the cases that have come under my notice, where such indefinite instruction has been given, the things have been planted in stiff blocks. Quite lately I came upon such an example in the garden of a friend who is by no means without a sense of beauty. There was a bank-like space on the outskirts of the pleasure-ground where it was wished to have a wild heath garden. A better place could hardly be, for the soil is light and sandy and the space lies out in full sunlight. The ground had been thrown about into ridges and valleys, but without any reference to its natural form, whereas with half the labour it might have been guided into slight hollows, ridges and promontories of good line and proportion. I found it planted with the path stiffly edged with one kind of heath on one side and another kind on the other; the back planting in rectangular blocks; near the front, bushes of *Hebe* at exactly even distances, and between each bush the same number of heaths in every interval quite stiffly planted. Some of the blocks at the back were of violets – plants quite unsuited to the place. Yet, only leaving out the violets, all the same plants might have been disposed so as to come quite easily and naturally. Then a thin sowing of the finer heath grasses, to include the pathway, where alone they would be mown, and a clever interplanting of wild thyme and the native wood sage (*Teucrium scorodonia*), common on the neighbouring heaths, would have put the whole thing together and would have given the impression, so desirable in wild planting, of the thing having so happened, rather than of its having been artificially made.

In planting or thinning trees also, the whole ultimate good of the effect will depend on this sense of form and good grouping. If these qualities are secured, the result in after years will be a poem; if they are neglected, it will be nothing but a crop.

I can imagine nothing more interesting than the guiding and part-planting of large stretches of natural young woodland, with some hilly ground above and water at the foot. As it is, I have to be content with my little wood of ten acres; yet I am truly glad to have even that small space to treat with reverent thankfulness and watchful care.

A spray of lavender.

Appendix I

GARDENS TO VISIT

Many readers of *Colour Schemes* will want to see examples of Miss Jekyll's work. Sadly, little remains of the garden at Munstead Wood and the same is true of many other Jekyll gardens. Fortunately there are exceptions. The jewel in the crown is Hestercombe in Somerset, restored after the discovery of Miss Jekyll's planting plans in a potting shed in 1973. At the Deanery in Berkshire, the pergola, patios and walls have been rebuilt and the planting delightfully reinstated. At Folly Farm, Sulhamstead, the restoration now extends to the wide herbaceous borders. Combend Manor in Gloucestershire has been substantially restored; and at Hascombe Court in Surrey – although the replanting has not adhered strictly to Jekyll plans – the great double herbaceous borders are perhaps the finest recreation of the scale of gardening practised by Miss Jekyll.

The influence of Gertrude Jekyll's ideas is easier to see. Hidcote Manor in Gloucestershire has the closest affinity to Munstead Wood with its colour borders and seasonal gardens. Sissinghurst in Kent, too, is renowned for its colour schemes, especially its White Garden. The blue gardens at Beningbrough are delightful examples of their kind, the juxtaposition of blue borders with twin borders of glowing reds and yellows at Chatsworth are stunning examples of what Miss Jekyll sought to achieve in her gardens of special colouring. There are fine herbaceous borders, one of strong colours and one of pastels, at Cliveden, and the grandeur of the larger Jekyll gardens is beautifully created at Hatfield House and Cranborne Manor. Bampton Manor in Oxfordshire has splendid double borders, which exemplify Miss Jekyll's softer colour schemes, and her combination of skillful planning and plantsmanship is reflected at Barnsley House, Gloucestershire.

Hestercombe can be visited by appointment, and the Deanery, Folly Farm and Combend are open on particular days through the National Gardens Scheme (although the Deanery is changing ownership). The other gardens are open regularly throughout the summer.

A SELECTION OF MISS JEKYLL'S GARDEN PLANS

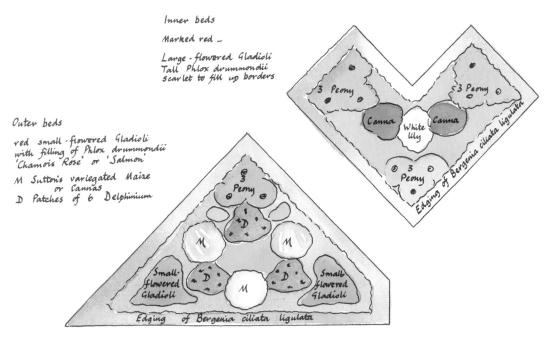

Inner beds

Marked red –

Large-flowered Gladioli
Tall Phlox drummondii
scarlet to fill up borders

Outer beds

red small-flowered Gladioli
with filling of Phlox drummondii
'Chamois Rose' or 'Salmon'

M Sutton's variegated Maize
or Cannas
D Patches of 6 Delphinium

3 Peony

3 Peony

Canna

White lily

Canna

3 Peony

Edging of Bergenia ciliata ligulata

3 Peony

M

M

D

Small-flowered Gladioli

D

M

D

Small-flowered Gladioli

Edging of Bergenia ciliata ligulata

Hestercombe, Somerset: The Great Plat (detail)

For the stone-edged beds of the 'Great Plat' at Hestercombe Miss
Jekyll designed a scheme which was at once bold and simple, graceful
and varied. The large leaves of bergenias matched the boldness of the
geometry but, by overgrowing the stone, simultaneously softened its
rigidity. Their early, dusky-pink flowers picked up the warm colouring
of the stone. As summer approached, peonies produced their heavy
blossoms, then they and the bergenias created the framework for the
rich colours of later summer – deep blue spires of delphiniums, cool
white and glowing orange lilies and large groups of scarlet and scarlet-
crimson gladioli. As the delphiniums faded and were cut down,
fountains of striped maize and striking clumps of cannas provided the
vertical emphasis.

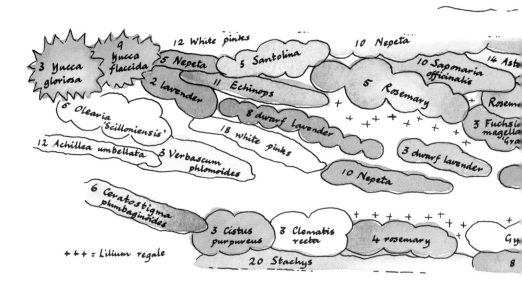

Hestercombe, Somerset: border and wall planting

At Hestercombe, Edwin Lutyens' bold design for the garden was sympathetically matched by Miss Jekyll's skill at planting. This plan shows two borders flanking a path on the upper level, then a retaining wall in rough-textured stone and finally a narrow, sun-baked border at the foot of the wall.

The upper borders were filled with grey foliage with a predominance of soft, grey-blue and dusky-pink flowers. Cloudy masses of gypsophila, nepeta, lavender, eryngiums, santolina and *Clematis heracleifolia* 'Davidiana' spilled over the path edged with stachys, pinks and *Cineraria maritima*. Tall clumps of globe thistles (*Echinops*) also provided blue flowers then acted as support for white perennial pea and *Clematis* 'Jackmanii' later in the season.

A similar range of plants emerged from crevices in the stonework to

drape the wall : stately verbascums here providing the yellow contrast
to the blues of santolina and phlomis in the upper borders. Many of
the plants in the upper borders and wall spilled down into the narrow
border below but they were supplemented by rounded bushes of cistus.

In the upper border, pale pink godetias provided annual flowers of
translucent delicacy at one end, while grey *Elymus* and pink soapwort
(both invasive weeds in many situations) concealed their ruthless
characters beneath a softly coloured harmony. In the wall it was the
groups of *Ceratostigma* at either end which provided surprise when its
foliage turned fiery crimson in late autumn to accompany its brilliant
blue flowers.

Above and below the wall, the arching and intensely fragrant
trumpets of *Lilium regale*, marked on the plan by small crosses, arched
out to impress their own beauty on the passer-by.

175

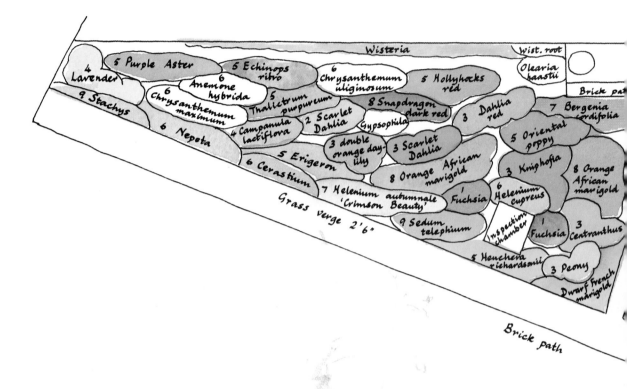

The Priory, Hitchin: south border
The south border at The Priory shows many similarities, on a smaller scale, to the main hardy flower border at Munstead Wood. At either end the colouring was soft blue and white, building up to yellow, orange and red in the middle. The background played an important role: at the eastern end, white hollyhocks, dahlias, anemones and other pale flowers showed up dramatically against the yew hedge and bold foliage of magnolia; the warm colours of the central border toned with the brick paths and walls of the house; at the western end, the softer colours faded into the grey-green foliage of wisterias.

Annuals were important, especially in the centre, where French and African marigolds, dahlias and antirrhinums provided much of the colour in the summer months when the oriental poppies, peonies and daylilies had completed their task.

176

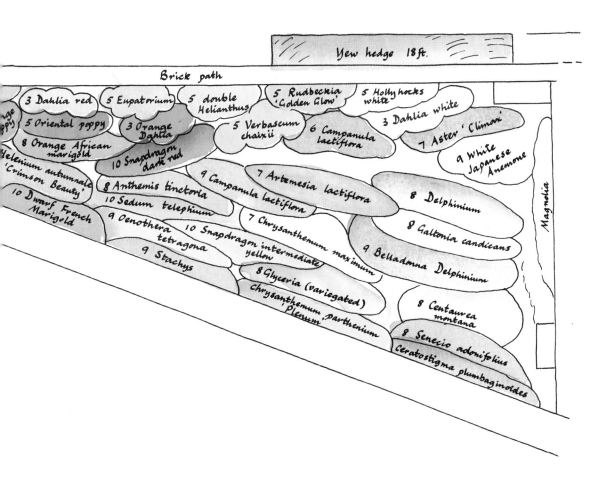

Yew hedge 18 ft.

Brick path

3 Dahlia red
5 Eupatorium
5 double Helianthus
5 Rudbeckia 'Golden Glow'
5 Hollyhocks white
5 Dahlia white
5 Oriental poppy
3 Orange Dahlia
5 Verbascum chaixii
6 Campanula lactiflora
3 Dahlia white
8 Orange African marigold
10 Snapdragon dark red
7 Aster 'Climax'
Helenium autumnale 'Crimson Beauty'
8 Anthemis tinctoria
9 Campanula lactiflora
7 Artemesia lactiflora
9 white Japanese Anemone
10 Dwarf French Marigold
10 Sedum telephium
8 Delphinium
9 Oenothera tetragona
10 Snapdragon intermediate yellow
7 Chrysanthemum maximum
8 Galtonia candicans
9 Stachys
8 Glyceria (variegated)
9 Belladonna Delphinium
Chrysanthemum Parthenium Plenum
8 Centaurea montana
8 Senecio adonifolius
Ceratostigma plumbaginoides
Magnolia

177

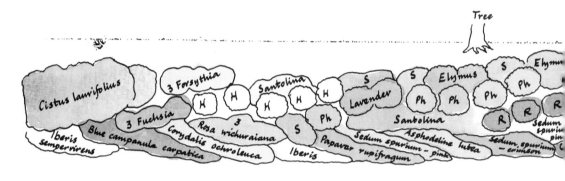

Crooksbury, Surrey : shady border

The shady border at Crooksbury — Lutyens' first major house and the first garden for which Miss Jekyll offered him advice — distills the cool refreshment of the woodland which she so loved. At the back, regularly spaced guelder rose (*Viburnum opulus*) were interplanted with *Clematis montana*, a combination of greenish and ivory white flowers which later featured large in the North Court of Munstead Wood. The end of the border was marked by skimmias, solid domes of glossy foliage and white flowers followed by red berries in winter. Strong colour was provided in spring and summer by oriental poppies and monarda but nearly all the other flowers were sharp yellow or soft white: aruncus, achillea, lupin, Solomon's seal, meadow sweet and *Chrysanthemum uliginosum*, yellow doronicum and evening primroses (*Oenothera*). Near the middle, delphiniums and spiderwort (*Tradescantia*) provided a note of clear blue among the yellow, and the border ended with softer grey-blues of asters and campanulas among the whites.

178

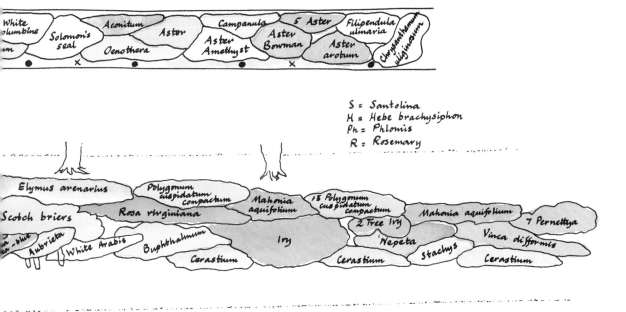

S = Santolina
H = Hebe brachysiphon
Ph = Phlomis
R = Rosemary

Chinthurst, Surrey : raised border

The plan for a bank at Chinthurst takes into account the dry, sandy soil, shade from trees and the south-westerly aspect. At the open end, santolina, lavender, phlomis, rosemary, cistus and hebe were woven into a tapestry of foliage colour ranging from almost white to almost black. Mounds of hebe were echoed by drifts of perennial candytuft (*Iberis sempervirens*) in the walls and the whole was prevented from becoming too rounded by cascading trails of *Rosa wichuraiana*. In the denser shade, tougher and softer plants were used : rosemary, Scotch briers and *Rosa virginiana*. Polygonum and mahonia provided rich colouring in autumn and winter.

The supporting wall carried iberis and arabis in spring, pinks, poppy, corydalis and campanula later, and finally the dusky colours of *Sedum spurium*. Cerastium, stachys, arabis and aubrieta added to the general greyness, except where a patch of ivy provided a more solid note below the tree ivies and mahonia in the deepest shade.

Appendix III
A NOTE ON MISS JEKYLL'S PLANT NAMES

No matter how much gardeners may fume and fret about it, the botanical names of plants are constantly changing. It is of no concern to the taxonomic botanist that the gardener must continually be altering his labels, or that the horticultural writer needs to be for ever updating his files; science moves inexorably onward. To those of us whose heads are not permanently buried among herbarium papers, only an imperfect impression can be gained of the imperatives that govern changes in plant nomenclature. It seems, however, that there are two main categories into which they fall; true advances in botanical knowledge, and the Law of Priority.

In the case of the former, modern scientific methods have greatly accelerated the process by which plants are placed into genera and species. Not least among these is the chromosome count – a weapon in the taxonomist's armoury whose dictates, given the present state of our knowledge, are incontrovertible. To put it simply, if a plant cannot be seen scientifically to belong to the genus or species to which it has previously been allocated, a nomenclatural change must follow and, usually, gardeners will accept it.

The Law of Priority is less easy to tolerate. To the layman it seems that teams of researchers with little better to do than to ferret endlessly among ancient papers occasionally surface gleefully to announce that author A ascribed a name to a plant a couple of years before author B gave it the name we all know and that therefore A's name must now enter the literature, while B's is reduced to the rank of synonymy.

In these ways it has come to pass that a very high proportion indeed of the botanical names that Gertrude Jekyll used have changed. Sometimes the genus is different, as in *Funkia* which is now *Hosta*, while in other instances it is the specific epithet that has been revised (*Magnolia conspicua*, for example, is now *M. denudata*). In other cases, both the generic name and the specific epithet are unrecognizable in the previous forms to modern gardeners.

It is name changes such as the one from *Agathaea coelestis* to *Felicia amelloides* that illustrate the justification for a comprehensive revision of the nomenclature used by Miss Jekyll. Only those with a large horticultural and botanical library would be able to read her original text with any true degree of comprehension, and whoever wanted to obtain a plant of *Spiraea lindleyana* would become involved in a great deal of research before finding out that it is *Sorbaria tomentosa*.

The modern trend in the horticultural trade is towards 'rationalization', which is to say that nurseries and garden centres – particularly the latter – tend to stock those plants for which there is a demand. Thus many plants become hard to find except in the stocks of specialist or dedicated nurserymen and women. Happily there is a sturdy band of such people, and what cannot be found with them of the plants mentioned by Miss Jekyll are almost all still in gardens and are circulated among gardeners, particularly among those who are members of the various plant societies.

It has not been necessary, therefore, to suggest alternatives for the plants that were available in Gertrude Jekyll's day. The only exception to this is among the *Dahlia* cultivars. Varieties of dahlias are rather ephemeral and have a tendency to disappear after just a few years because of disease or over-propagation. The modern gardener might, in fact, do almost as well by growing bedding dahlias cheaply from seed and choosing the colours required in particular settings.

Just occasionally I have proposed that plants different from Miss Jekyll's suggestions be grown. One such is *Olearia* 'Scilloniensis'. She cites *O. gunnii* – a mistake, in fact, as it was then known as *O. gunniana*. This plant now bears the name *O. phlogopappa* but it is for reasons of horticultural desirability and not merely to avoid this hideous burden that I have revised it to the far better plant which has now completely superseded it in gardens.

Similarly, *Caryopteris* × *clandonensis* is universally grown in place of *C. mastacanthus*, which is now *C. incana*. The hybrid vigour of *C.* × *clandonensis*, resulting from the species being crossed with *C. mongolica*, has endowed it with qualities that make it a superior garden plant.

Gardeners are very conservative indeed and it may be a very long time before they consent to adopt changes made by botanists. Gertrude Jekyll herself was using many names that had been dropped by taxonomists for many years. It would, therefore, be pedantic and perhaps confusing if some plants which are universally popular and well-known by their older names were to be updated. Everyone speaks of *Lithospermum diffusum* (usually the variety 'Heavenly Blue'). This plant has in its time been *L. prostratum* (as Miss Jekyll had it), *Lithodora prostrata*, and *Lithodora diffusa*. Priority now dictates that this last name is the valid one, but I suspect that gardeners will hang on to their present practice until the wheel comes full circle.

The present-day convention governing the writing of Latin plant names is that all specific epithets, no matter what their derivations, shall be written with lower-case initial letters. Previously, those derived from proper names were given capital initials. Miss Jekyll was, like many of her contemporaries, very inconsistent about this and wrote both *Daphne Mezereum* and *Euphorbia Wulfenii*, while inexplicably rendering a cistus as *C. cyprius*. In this edition, the modern way has been followed.

When is comes to the writing of the vernacular names for plants we find ourselves in a rapidly changing situation. Miss Jekyll would write 'Oak' or 'Ash' with capitals, whereas we dispense with them. Until very recently, however, the convention was to regard 'Red Oak' or 'Mountain Ash' as proper nouns and to honour them with capitals, but this is quickly being abandoned, as it is very difficult to be consistent. Similarly, English names for wild flowers are no longer being written as Lily-of-the-Valley, Cranesbill, etc, but as lily-of-the-valley, and so on. In decapitalizing all vernacular names, I have made but one exception: proper names in vernacular plant names should, I believe, remain, as in Solomon's seal.

If the spirit and rhythm of Gertrude Jekyll's writing is not to be interfered with in effecting the modernization of the nomenclature in it, then pedantry must be avoided. Her style permits 'Madame Alfred Carrière roses' and it suits the context better than the more correct "plants of *Rosa* 'Madame Alfred Carrière'." On the other hand, the very occasional sentence has had to be changed when she is mentioning synonyms that no longer have any meaning. On the whole, though, Miss Jekyll's message should now have as much meaning to modern gardeners as it did to her contemporaries.

John Kelly

INDEX

NOTES

1   *Narcissus nanus* of gardens is now regarded as *N. minor* var. *conspicuus*.
2   *Narcissus pallidiflorus* is, strictly, a Pyrenean form of the Tenby daffodil, *N. pseudo-narcissus*.
3   These tree peonies are no longer available in commerce: substitute 'Raphael' (warm flesh pink) for 'Comtesse de Tuder' and 'Lord Selbourne' (pale salmon pink) for 'Elizabeth'.
4   *Iris cengialti* is still grown, but seldom; a good blue Intermediate iris would be a suitable alternative.
5   *Geranium* × *magnificum* is grown today in preference to *G. platypetalum*.
6   Plants of the Belladonna Section of *Delphinium* are little grown nowadays, although their qualities are sufficiently appreciated for them to be cultivated by members of the horticultural trade. 'Blue Bees' has been a favourite for many years, and the best dark Oxford-blue variety is probably 'Wendy'.
7   For example, *Tradescantia virginiana* 'J.C. Weguelin'.
8   These named dahlias grown in Miss Jekyll's day no longer exist. A specialist dahlia nursery will advise on modern varieties of equivalent colour.
9   *Amaranthus paniculatus* var. *cruentus*.
10 Miss Jekyll's *Aster umbellatus* was probably *A. amygdalinus*.
11 *Helianthus* 'Miss Mellish' is now almost impossible to obtain, but the pale yellow varieties available today (such as 'Capenoch Star' and 'Soleil d'Or') are consistent with Miss Jekyll's reluctance to use orange tones in the gold scheme.
12 This rose is botanically *R. glauca* – although the name has little currency among gardeners, to whom it is universally *R. rubrifolia* now.

ACKNOWLEDGEMENTS

Frances Lincoln Ltd would like to thank the following individuals for their help: Susan Berry, Penny David and Sarah Mitchell for editorial direction and administration; Richard Bisgrove of Reading University for expert horticultural and historical contributions; Margaret Cawkwell for the index; Anne Fraser for picture research; Caroline Hillier and Anne Wilson for design direction and administration; and John Kelly for botanical advice. Charlotte Wess would like to thank the following for help in producing the illustrations for this book: The Royal Horticultural Society, Wisley, and the Curator John Main and his staff, among them Adrian Whitely and, in particular, Peter Barnes; The Chelsea Physic Garden, London and the Curator Duncan Donald; and especially William Scott for encouragement and support throughout the project.

All the photographs were taken specially for this book by Jerry Harpur (© Frances Lincoln Ltd), except the following: Agence Photographique TOP/ Robert Cesar 112; Inge Espen-Hansen 30; Elizabeth Whiting & Associates/Karl-Dietrich Bühler 65; Marijke Heuff 133; Jerry Harpur 43, 46, 56, 82, 98, 103, 134, 138, 162, 165, 167; Georges Lévêque 20, 75, 85, 110, 115, 143; S & O Mathews 90; Tania Midgley 119; Natural Image/Bob Gibbons 145; Hugh Palmer 34; Clay Perry 87; Gary Rogers 154.

Special thanks to Mary Dachowski for the plan artwork and calligraphy.